Creating Gems with Gemini

with Gemini

Mastering the Art of AI Interaction

By Laurence Lars Svekis

Dedicated to

Alexis and Sebastian

Thank you for your support

For more content and to learn more, visit
https://basescripts.com

Chapter 1: Introduction to Gemini 8

Learning Objectives 8

What is Gemini? (Large Language Models Explained Simply)...8

Overview of Capabilities 9

The "Gem" Philosophy: Defining Valuable AI Output 11

Setting the Stage: Why Skillful Interaction Matters..........12

Exercises & Action Items 13

Chapter 1 Checklist...14

Chapter 2: The Language of Interaction - How Gemini Understands You 15

Learning Objectives 15

Natural Language Processing (NLP) Basics for Users 16

Tokens, Context Windows, and Their Impact....................17

How Gemini Processes Prompts and Generates Responses 18

Understanding Biases and Limitations.................................19

Exercises & Action Items 20

Chapter 2 Checklist...22

Learning Objectives 24

Accessing and Using the Gemini Interface(s) 24

Essential Settings and Configurations (If Applicable)......26

Keeping Track of Your Interactions and "Gems" 27

Exercises & Action Items 28

Chapter 3 Checklist...30

Chapter 4: The Anatomy of a Great Prompt..........................31

Clarity and Specificity: Being Direct 32

Context is King: Providing Necessary Background..........34

Defining the Desired Output: Format, Tone, Style, Length 36

Constraints and Instructions: Guiding the AI 38

Putting It All Together: An Example of a Great Prompt..40

Sample Exercises 41

Action Items...41

Checklist: The Anatomy of a Great Prompt.......................42

Chapter 5: Basic Prospecting Techniques..............................43

Asking Effective Questions 44

Requesting Summaries and Explanations...........................45

Generating Lists and Outlines 47

Simple Creative Prompts (poems, short descriptions).....48

Putting It All Together: An Example 50

Sample Exercises 50

Action Items...51

Checklist: Basic Prospecting Techniques...........................51

Chapter 6: Advanced Prospecting - Refining Your Approach 53

Iterative Prompting: Refining Results Step-by-Step 54

Role-Playing: Assigning a Persona to Gemini 56

Few-Shot Prompting: Providing Examples.........................58

Chain-of-Thought Prompting: Encouraging Reasoning ..59

Negative Prompts: Specifying What Not to Include 61

Putting It All Together: Combining Advanced Techniques 62

Sample Exercises 62

Action Items...63

Checklist: Advanced Prospecting - Refining Your Approach...63

Chapter 7: Crafting Brilliant Text 65

Writing and Editing Assistance (Grammar, Style, Clarity) 66

Generating Different Forms: Essays, Articles, Reports, Emails 68

Creative Writing: Stories, Scripts, Poetry 70

Marketing and Communication Copy................................71

Putting It All Together: Crafting a Blog Post....................73

Sample Exercises 74

Action Items..74

Checklist: Crafting Brilliant Text 75

Chapter 8: Mining for Code..77

Generating Code Snippets in Various Languages 78

Explaining Code and Concepts...80

Debugging Assistance 82

Translating Code Between Languages 83

Best Practices for AI-Assisted Coding 85

Putting It All Together: Generating and Understanding a Simple Program..85

Sample Exercises 86

Action Items...86

Checklist: Mining for Code...87

Chapter 9: Unearthing Insights - Data Analysis and Interpretation..88

Summarizing Complex Information 89

Generating Hypotheses..92

Explaining Technical Concepts Simply 94

Putting It All Together: Analyzing Customer Reviews ...95

Sample Exercises 97

Action Items..97

Checklist: Unearthing Insights - Data Analysis and
Interpretation...98

Chapter 10: Designing and Brainstorming............................99

Generating Ideas for Projects, Products, Content 100

Creating Outlines and Structures 103

Developing User Personas and Scenarios 106

Assisting with Visual Concepts (describing layouts,
themes) 108

Putting It All Together: Planning a Weekend Event 110

Sample Exercises 111

Action Items..111

Checklist: Designing and Brainstorming...........................112

Chapter 11: Combining Tools - Gemini in Your Workflow
....113

Integrating Gemini with other software and tools..........114

Using Gemini for research assistance (fact-checking
required!)...117

Automating repetitive tasks (conceptual) 118

Putting It All Together: A Day in the Life with Gemini.119

Sample Exercises 120

Action Items..121

Checklist: Combining Tools - Gemini in Your Workflow
....121

Chapter 12: The Ethics of AI Gem Creation 123

Understanding plagiarism and originality 124

Bias detection and mitigation in outputs 126

Responsible use of AI-generated content 127

Transparency and disclosure 129

Putting It All Together: Ethical Considerations in Action 130

Sample Exercises 131

Action Items...131

Checklist: The Ethics of AI Gem Creation........................132

Chapter 13: Troubleshooting - When the Mine Runs Dry .133

Dealing with generic or unhelpful responses..................134

Recognizing and working around limitations.................136

Adjusting prompts when stuck 138

Putting It All Together: Troubleshooting a Recipe Request 139

Sample Exercises 140

Action Items...140

Chapter 14: The Future of Gemini and AI Collaboration ..142

Emerging capabilities 143

The evolving role of AI in creativity and productivity ..145

Lifelong learning: Staying updated..................................146

Final Thoughts...148

Action Items...148

Checklist: The Future of Gemini and AI Collaboration .148

Test Your Knowledge...150

Appendix A: Prompt Library Sampler (Examples for Various Tasks) 188

Appendix B: Glossary of AI and Gemini Terms..................195

Conclusion - Your Journey to Becoming a Gemini Gem Creator 201

Chapter 1: Introduction to Gemini

Welcome! You're about to embark on an exciting journey into the world of Gemini, a powerful tool that can help you create amazing things. Think of this book as your guide and Gemini as your collaborator. Together, we'll learn how to move beyond simple questions and answers to craft truly valuable outputs – what we'll call "gems." This first chapter is all about getting acquainted with Gemini and understanding the potential that awaits.

Learning Objectives

By the end of this chapter, you will be able to:

- Explain in simple terms what a Large Language Model (LLM) is.
- Describe what Gemini is and who created it.
- List several key capabilities of Gemini (what it can *do*).
- Understand the "Gem" philosophy: what makes an AI output truly valuable.
- Recognize why your interaction and prompts are crucial for getting great results from Gemini.

What is Gemini? (Large Language Models Explained Simply)

Have you ever used autocomplete on your phone or email? It tries to predict the next word you want to type. Now, imagine that capability supercharged – massively supercharged! That gives you a tiny glimpse into the world of Large Language Models, or LLMs.

An LLM is a type of Artificial Intelligence (AI) trained on enormous amounts of text and code data from the internet and digital books. By processing all this information, it learns patterns, structures, grammar, facts, reasoning styles, and even coding languages. It becomes incredibly good at understanding and generating human-like text.

Think of it like an incredibly well-read assistant who has digested more books, articles, and websites than any human ever could. It doesn't "think" or "feel" like a human, but it can process your requests (your "prompts") and generate relevant, coherent, and often very helpful text in response.

Gemini is the name for a family of powerful LLMs developed by Google. It's designed to be multimodal, meaning it can understand and work with different types of information, like text, code, images, and audio (though our focus in this book will primarily be on text and code interactions). When you interact with Gemini, you're tapping into one of the most advanced LLMs available today.

In simple terms: Gemini is a sophisticated AI from Google that understands your text instructions and generates text-based responses, drawing on the vast knowledge it was trained on.

Overview of Capabilities

**So, what can this "incredibly well-read assistant"
actually *do*?** Gemini is versatile! Here are some of the core things you can ask Gemini to help you with:

- **Answering Questions: From simple facts ("What is the capital of France?"**) to complex explanations ("Explain the concept of photosynthesis in simple terms.").

- Generating Text: Writing emails, drafting reports, creating stories, composing poems, generating marketing copy, writing blog posts, and much more.
- Summarizing Information: Condensing long articles, research papers, or meeting notes into key points.
- Translating Languages: Converting text from one language to another.
- Generating Code: Writing code snippets in various programming languages (like Python, JavaScript, HTML), explaining code, or even helping debug errors.
- Brainstorming Ideas: Coming up with ideas for projects, gifts, party themes, business names, or creative storylines.
- Analyzing and Explaining: Breaking down complex topics, explaining concepts, or identifying pros and cons.
- Editing and Proofreading: Helping you refine your own writing for clarity, grammar, and style.

Simple Examples:

- **Asking a question: What are the main benefits of regular exercise?**
- Generating text: Write a short, friendly email reminding my team about Friday's meeting.
- Summarizing: Summarize the main points of this article [you might paste text here in a real interaction].
- Brainstorming: Give me 5 ideas for a fantasy short story.

This is just the tip of the iceberg. As you learn to interact more skillfully, you'll discover even more ways Gemini can assist you.

The "Gem" Philosophy: Defining Valuable AI Output

You can ask Gemini a simple question and get a simple answer. That's useful, but it's not necessarily a "gem." In this book, when we talk about creating "gems" with Gemini, we mean generating outputs that are:

- High-Quality: Well-written, accurate (to the best of the AI's knowledge), coherent, and relevant.
- Insightful: Offering a perspective, analysis, or connection you might not have thought of yourself.
- Creative: Producing novel ideas, unique expressions, or imaginative content.
- Useful & Actionable: Directly helping you solve a problem, complete a task, or achieve a specific goal.
- Tailored: Perfectly matching the specific format, tone, style, and requirements you set out in your prompt.

Think of the difference between finding a common pebble on the beach and finding a polished, sparkling gemstone. Both are stones, but the gemstone has unique qualities that make it stand out – it has been shaped, refined, and possesses a certain brilliance.

A "gem" output from Gemini isn't just *any* response; it's a response that truly shines because it perfectly meets (or even exceeds) your needs, born from a thoughtful interaction. It's the difference between asking Tell me about dogs and getting a generic paragraph, versus asking Write a heartwarming short story from the perspective of an old golden retriever waiting for his owner to come home, focusing on sounds and smells and getting a piece of creative writing that resonates emotionally. The second output, tailored and specific, is closer to being a "gem."

Setting the Stage: Why Skillful Interaction Matters

Gemini is an incredibly powerful tool, but it's still a tool. Like a hammer, a paintbrush, or a musical instrument, the quality of the result depends heavily on the skill of the person using it.

You can't just vaguely wave a paintbrush at a canvas and expect a masterpiece. Similarly, you can't just give Gemini vague or poorly constructed prompts and expect "gems" every time.

Your prompts – the instructions, questions, and context you provide – are the key.

- **Clarity: Does Gemini understand exactly what you're asking for?**
- **Context: Does it have the necessary background information?**
- **Specificity: Have you defined the desired output format, tone, length, and style?**
- **Guidance: Have you given it constraints or examples to steer it in the right direction?**

Learning to communicate effectively with Gemini – learning the art of prompt engineering – is how you transform its potential into polished gems. The better you become at asking, guiding, and refining your interactions, the more insightful, creative, and useful its outputs will be.

That's what this book is all about: equipping you with the knowledge and techniques to become a skillful Gemini user, capable of consistently creating your own AI-generated gems.

Exercises & Action Items

Let's dip our toes in the water! Don't worry about crafting perfect prompts yet; this is just about starting the conversation.

Sample Exercise 1: Ask a Fact

- Go to your Gemini interface.
- Ask it a simple factual question. **Examples: What is the highest mountain in the world? or Who invented the telephone?**
- Observe the response. **Is it clear? Does it directly answer your question?**

Sample Exercise 2: Request a Simple Creative Piece

- Ask Gemini to write something very short and creative. Examples: Write a four-line poem about rain. or Tell me a one-sentence joke.
- Look at the result. **Does it follow the instructions?**

Action Item 1: Explore Capabilities

- Think of three different types of tasks from the "Overview of Capabilities" section (e.g., summarizing, brainstorming, writing an email).
- Try asking Gemini to perform a very simple version of each task. For example:
  - Summarize this sentence: The quick brown fox jumps over the lazy dog.
  - Give me one idea for a healthy breakfast.
  - Write a one-sentence email saying thank you.
- Get a feel for how it responds to different kinds of requests.

Action Item 2: Reflect on the "Gem" Idea

- Think about a recent task you did (writing something, solving a problem, looking for information).

- **How might a truly *excellent*, insightful, or perfectly tailored AI response (a "gem") have helped you with that task? What would that ideal response have looked like?**

Chapter 1 Checklist

Use this checklist to ensure you've grasped the key concepts from this chapter:

[ ] I can explain that an LLM is an AI trained on lots of text to understand and generate language.

[ ] I know that Gemini is Google's LLM.

[ ] I can name at least 3 different things Gemini can do (e.g., answer questions, write text, generate code).

[ ] I understand that a "gem" output is high-quality, insightful, creative, useful, and tailored – not just any response.

[ ] I recognize that the quality of my prompts and interaction directly impacts the quality of Gemini's output.

[ ] I have tried at least one simple interaction with Gemini.

Congratulations on completing Chapter 1! You've taken the first crucial step. You now have a foundational understanding of what Gemini is and why learning to interact with it skillfully is so important for creating those valuable "gems." Keep this foundation in mind as we move forward.

Chapter 2: The Language of Interaction - How Gemini Understands You

Welcome back! In Chapter 1, we got acquainted with Gemini and the exciting idea of creating "gems." Now, let's peek behind the curtain a little. **How does Gemini actually understand what you type? How does it turn your prompts into coherent, relevant responses?** Understanding this process, even at a basic level, is incredibly helpful for learning how to communicate effectively with Gemini. Think of it like learning the basic grammar of a new language – it helps you express yourself more clearly.

Learning Objectives

By the end of this chapter, you will be able to:

- Explain the basic idea behind Natural Language Processing (NLP) in the context of AI.
- Define what "tokens" are and why they matter for Gemini.
- Understand the concept of a "context window" and how it affects your interactions.
- Describe the simplified process of how Gemini likely handles your prompts.
- Identify potential biases and limitations in AI responses and understand why critical evaluation is important.

Natural Language Processing (NLP) Basics for Users

At its heart, Gemini works using something called Natural Language Processing, or NLP. Don't let the technical term scare you! It's simply the field of AI focused on enabling computers to understand, interpret, and generate human language – the way *you* naturally speak and write.

Imagine teaching a computer language like you might teach a child. You start with letters, then words, then sentence structures, meanings, and context. NLP involves sophisticated techniques that allow AI like Gemini to:

1. Read: Process the text you input.
2. Understand: Figure out the meaning, intent, and key information in your text.
3. Generate: Create new text that is grammatically correct, relevant, and coherent based on its understanding and training.

Why does this matter to you? Because knowing that Gemini is trying to *process* your *natural language* helps you understand that clarity and structure in your prompts are important. Just like speaking clearly helps another person understand you better, writing clear prompts helps Gemini understand you better.

Simple Example:

If you tell a friend, "Get me that thing over there," they might be confused. **What thing? Where?**

If you say, "Please pass me the blue book on the coffee table," they know exactly what you mean.

Similarly, clear, specific language helps Gemini grasp your request accurately.

Tokens, Context Windows, and Their Impact

Okay, let's get slightly more specific, but still keep it simple. When Gemini processes your prompt, it doesn't see whole words or sentences exactly as we do. It breaks the text down into smaller pieces called tokens.

A token might be a whole word (like "hello" or "book"), a part of a word (like "ing" or "process"), a punctuation mark, or even a space. Think of tokens as the basic building blocks Gemini uses for language.

Example Tokenization (Simplified):

The sentence: Gemini understands text.

Might become tokens like: ["Gem", "ini", " under", "stands", " text", "."]

Why do tokens matter? Because they relate directly to something called the context window.

The context window is like Gemini's short-term memory for a specific conversation. It represents the maximum number of tokens Gemini can consider at one time – this includes both your prompt and its own response so far in that chat session.

Imagine you can only hold five LEGO bricks in your hand at once. If someone gives you a sixth brick, you have to drop one of the earlier ones. The context window is similar. If a conversation gets too long (exceeds the token limit of the context window), Gemini might start to "forget" the very beginning of the conversation or prompt.

Impact on You:

- Very Long Prompts: If your prompt is extremely long, parts of it might fall outside the context window, and Gemini might not consider the earliest instructions.
- Long Conversations: In a lengthy back-and-forth chat, Gemini might lose track of details mentioned much earlier.
- Efficiency: Shorter, more concise prompts use fewer tokens and fit easily within the context window.

You don't usually need to count tokens precisely, but understanding the concept helps explain why sometimes breaking down a very complex request into smaller parts, or starting a new chat for a completely new topic, can be beneficial.

How Gemini Processes Prompts and Generates Responses

So, what happens when you hit "Enter" after typing your prompt? Here's a simplified look at the likely process:

1. Tokenization: Gemini breaks your prompt down into tokens (those building blocks we just discussed).
2. Understanding (Encoding): It analyzes these tokens, considering their meaning, the relationships between them, and the overall context, trying to grasp your intent based on its vast training data.
3. Prediction (Decoding): This is where the magic seems to happen. Based on its understanding of your prompt and everything it learned during training, Gemini starts predicting the most likely sequence of tokens to come next. It predicts one token, then the next, then the next, essentially building its response piece by piece. It's like predicting the next word in a sentence, but on a much more complex level.

4. Response Generation: It assembles these predicted tokens back into human-readable text – the response you see on your screen.

Think of it like a musician hearing the first few notes of a very familiar song. Based on those notes and their knowledge of music, they can predict how the rest of the melody is likely to go. Gemini does something similar with language, predicting the sequence of tokens based on the "notes" (your prompt) it receives.

Understanding Biases and Limitations

Gemini is powerful, but it's not perfect. It's crucial to be aware of its potential biases and limitations.

Biases:

Because LLMs like Gemini learn from vast amounts of text written by humans (from the internet, books, etc.), they can unfortunately absorb the biases present in that text. This might include:

- Stereotypes: Reflecting unfair assumptions about groups of people based on gender, race, nationality, profession, etc.
- Skewed Perspectives: Over-representing certain viewpoints found more commonly in the training data.

Example: If the training data contained many texts describing nurses as female and doctors as male, the AI might inadvertently default to these stereotypes in its responses unless prompted otherwise.

Limitations:

- No True Understanding: Gemini doesn't "understand" concepts or "know" things in the human sense. It's pattern-matching and predicting text sequences.
- Potential for Inaccuracy ("Hallucinations"): Sometimes, Gemini might generate text that sounds plausible but is factually incorrect or nonsensical. It might "make things up" to fill gaps in its knowledge or satisfy the prompt's structure. Always critically evaluate information, especially for important decisions.
- Knowledge Cutoff: Its knowledge is generally limited to the information available up to its last training date. It might not know about very recent events or developments.
- Lack of Common Sense: It might struggle with reasoning that requires real-world experience or common sense understanding.
- Can Be Overly Confident: It often presents information very confidently, even when it's incorrect.

Why this Matters: Don't treat Gemini's output as infallible truth. Always apply your own judgment, cross-reference critical information with reliable sources, and be mindful of potential biases. You are still in control!

Exercises & Action Items

Let's apply these concepts.

Sample Exercise 1: Testing NLP Understanding

- Ask Gemini to explain a relatively complex term in simple words. Example: Explain "photosynthesis" like I'm 10 years old.
- **Observe: Does the explanation make sense? Is it appropriately simple?** This tests its ability to process your request for simplification.

Sample Exercise 2: Probing the Context Window (Conceptual)

- Write a short prompt with two distinct instructions at the beginning. Then add a few sentences of unrelated filler text. Finally, ask Gemini to perform both initial instructions. Example:
1. Tell me a joke. 2. **What is the capital of Australia?** Filler text: The weather today is nice, I hope it stays sunny. I need to remember to buy milk later. Okay, now do tasks 1 and 2.
- **Observe: Does it remember and perform *both* initial tasks?** (Note: Context windows are usually quite large, so this simple test might still work, but it illustrates the concept).

Sample Exercise 3: Checking for Limitations

- Ask Gemini about a very recent major world event (something that happened *yesterday* or *today*). **Example: What were the major global headlines from today, [Insert Today's Date]?**
- **Observe: Does it provide accurate, up-to-the-minute information, or does it state its knowledge cutoff?** This highlights the knowledge limitation.

Action Item 1: Practice Rephrasing

- Take a simple request you made in Chapter 1 (like asking for a poem).
- Try asking for the *same thing* but phrase your prompt differently three times.
- Notice if the responses change based on your phrasing. This reinforces how Gemini processes natural language variations.

Action Item 2: Critical Evaluation Practice

- Ask Gemini a question about a topic you know reasonably well.
- Review the answer carefully. **Is it completely accurate? Is there any nuance missing? Does it seem biased in any way?** Get in the habit of questioning the output.

Action Item 3: Breaking Down Requests

- Think of a complex task (e.g., planning a detailed weekend trip itinerary).
- Instead of asking for everything at once, try breaking it down into smaller prompts (e.g., "Suggest 3 destinations," then "List family-friendly activities in [chosen destination]," then "Draft a possible schedule"). Reflect on whether this feels easier for Gemini to handle (and potentially avoids context window issues).

Chapter 2 Checklist

Review this checklist to solidify your understanding:

[ ] I understand that NLP is how AI like Gemini processes and understands human language.

[ ] I can explain that "tokens" are small pieces of text (like words or parts of words) that Gemini uses.

[ ] I know the "context window" is like Gemini's short-term memory, limiting how much text it can consider at once.

[ ] I have a basic idea of how Gemini processes prompts: Tokenize -> Understand -> Predict -> Generate Response.

[ ] I am aware that Gemini's responses can sometimes contain biases inherited from training data.

[ ] I recognize key limitations, such as potential inaccuracies ("hallucinations") and knowledge cutoffs.

[ ] I understand the importance of critically evaluating Gemini's outputs and not taking them as absolute truth.

Great job working through Chapter 2! Understanding these background concepts – how Gemini "hears" and "speaks" – empowers you to interact more effectively. You're building the foundation needed to start crafting truly skillful prompts, which is exactly where we're heading next.

Chapter 3: Setting Up Your Workspace

Now that we've explored what Gemini is and how it understands language, it's time to get practical. **Where do you actually *go* to interact with Gemini? How do you keep track of the conversations and the brilliant "gems" you'll soon be creating?** This chapter is all about setting up your digital workspace – finding your way around the Gemini interface and developing habits for organizing your interactions. Think of it as preparing your workbench before starting a creative project.

Learning Objectives

By the end of this chapter, you will be able to:

- Identify the common ways to access and interact with Gemini.
- Describe the basic components of a typical Gemini interface (input area, response area, history).
- Understand the importance of keeping track of your prompts and Gemini's responses.
- List several simple methods for organizing and saving your interactions and "gems."
- Feel comfortable navigating the basic Gemini environment you are using.

Accessing and Using the Gemini Interface(s)

Gemini isn't a physical thing you can hold; it's software you access through a digital interface. Google provides several ways to interact with Gemini, and these might evolve over time. Common access points often include:

- Web Interface: A dedicated website where you can type prompts and receive responses directly in your browser. This is often the most common starting point.
- Mobile App: A dedicated app for your smartphone or tablet, allowing you to use Gemini on the go.
- Integrations: Gemini might also be integrated into other Google products or third-party applications (though we'll focus on the direct interfaces for now).

Regardless of *how* you access it, the core interaction usually looks similar. You'll typically find:

1. Input Area: A text box, often at the bottom or top of the screen, where you type your prompt (your instructions or questions for Gemini).
2. Send/Submit Button: A button (often looking like a paper airplane or simply saying "Send") that you click after typing your prompt.
3. Response Area: The main part of the screen where Gemini's generated text appears after you send your prompt.
4. Chat History/Conversation List: Usually somewhere on the side or accessible via a menu, this area shows your previous conversations or prompts within the current session or across sessions. This lets you revisit past interactions.

Using the Interface - The Basic Flow:

It's usually as simple as this:

1. Navigate to the Gemini web interface or open the app.
2. Locate the input area.
3. Type your prompt (e.g., **What's a simple recipe for chocolate chip cookies?**).
4. Click the Send/Submit button.

5. Wait a few moments while Gemini processes your request.
6. Read the response that appears in the response area.

That's it! You've had your first (or maybe just your most recent) conversation with Gemini.

Essential Settings and Configurations (If Applicable)

Most Gemini interfaces are designed to be straightforward, especially for beginners. While there might be some settings available, the most crucial element for getting good results is the quality of your prompts, which we'll focus on heavily in upcoming chapters.

Depending on the specific interface you're using, you *might* find settings related to:

- Account Management: Standard settings related to your Google account.
- Appearance: Options like light mode or dark mode for visual preference.
- History Management: Settings for managing or deleting your past conversations.

For the purpose of learning to create "gems," you generally don't need to worry too much about complex configurations at the start. The default settings are usually fine. The main "configuration" you'll be doing is crafting effective prompts! If specific settings become relevant to advanced techniques later, we'll address them then. For now, focus on getting comfortable with the basic interaction flow.

Keeping Track of Your Interactions and "Gems"

As you start experimenting, you'll quickly realize that some prompts work much better than others. You'll generate responses that are particularly insightful, creative, or useful – your first "gems"! It's incredibly helpful to have a system for saving and organizing these valuable interactions. **Why?**

- Learning: Revisiting successful prompts helps you understand what works.
- Re-use: You might want to use a similar prompt structure again for a different task.
- Refinement: You can look back at less successful attempts and see how you could improve the prompt.
- Reference: Easily find that brilliant idea or useful piece of information Gemini generated for you last week.

Here are a few simple methods to keep track:

1. Leverage Built-in History: Most interfaces keep a history of your recent chats. Get familiar with how to access and navigate this history. You can often rename chats to make them easier to find later (e.g., "Brainstorming Blog Post Ideas," "Python Code Examples").
2. Copy and Paste: The simplest method! When you get a prompt/response pair you like, copy the text and paste it into a separate document. This could be:
   - A simple text file (.txt)
   - A document in a word processor (like Google Docs, Microsoft Word)
   - A note-taking app (like Google Keep, Evernote, Apple Notes)
   - Organize these notes with clear titles or folders.

3. Spreadsheet Log: For a more structured approach, create a simple spreadsheet (using Google Sheets, Microsoft Excel, etc.). You could have columns for:
   - Date
   - Goal/Task
   - Your Prompt
   - Gemini's Response (or key parts of it)
   - **Notes/Rating (How well did it work?**)
4. Dedicated Notebook: If you prefer physical notes, keep a dedicated notebook where you write down your best prompts and summarize the key takeaways from the responses.

The best system is the one you'll actually use consistently. Start simple and adapt as you go. The key is to make it easy to save and find your valuable interactions.

Exercises & Action Items

Time to get familiar with your workspace!

Sample Exercise 1: Interface Navigation

- Open the Gemini interface you plan to use (web or app).
- Identify the input area. Type Hello, Gemini! and press Send/Submit.
- Identify the response area where the answer appears.
- Locate your chat history. Can you see the "Hello, Gemini!" **interaction listed?** If possible, try renaming this test chat to something like "My First Test".

Sample Exercise 2: Saving an Interaction

- **Ask Gemini a simple question, like** What are three common types of house plants?

- Once you get the response, practice copying both your prompt and Gemini's full response.
- Paste this copied text into a place you choose for saving notes (a new text file, a Google Doc, a note in an app). Give it a clear title like "House Plant Info".

Action Item 1: Explore Your Interface

- Spend 5-10 minutes clicking around the Gemini interface you are using. Don't worry about prompting complex things yet. Just see what menus or options are available. Look for any settings related to appearance or history, but don't feel obligated to change anything.

Action Item 2: Choose Your Tracking Method

- Consider the tracking methods listed (history, copy-paste, spreadsheet, notebook).
- Decide which method (or combination) seems most practical for you *right now*.
- Set up your chosen system. If it's copy-pasting, create a dedicated folder or document. If it's a spreadsheet, create the file and add the column headers.

Action Item 3: Save Your First "Potential Gem"

- Think back to any previous interactions you've had (maybe from exercises in Chapters 1 or 2).
- **Was there any response you found particularly interesting, helpful, or well-written?**
- If so, try to find it in your history (if possible) or recreate the prompt.
- Save this prompt/response pair using the tracking method you chose in Action Item 2. Label it clearly. This is the start of your personal "gem" collection!

Chapter 3 Checklist

Use this checklist to confirm you're comfortable with your workspace:

[ ] I know how to access the Gemini interface I will be using (web, app, etc.).

[ ] I can easily find the input box, send button, and response area.

[ ] I know how to find my chat history (if available).

[ ] I understand why saving good prompts and responses is beneficial.

[ ] I have chosen at least one method for tracking my interactions (e.g., history, copy-paste, spreadsheet).

[ ] I have practiced saving at least one prompt/response pair.

Excellent! You've now set up your workspace and have a plan for organizing your journey. Having a comfortable environment and a way to track your progress and successes makes the learning process much smoother. You're ready to move on to the core skill of crafting effective prompts!

Chapter 4: The Anatomy of a Great Prompt

Welcome to Chapter 4! By now, you've likely had some initial interactions with Gemini and are starting to see its potential. In this chapter, we're going to delve into the heart of effective AI interaction: **the prompt**. Think of a prompt as your set of instructions to Gemini. Just like a skilled chef needs a clear recipe to create a delicious dish, Gemini needs a well-crafted prompt to generate the high-quality "gems" you're looking for.

This chapter will break down the essential components of a great prompt. We'll explore how to communicate your needs clearly, provide the necessary background information, and guide Gemini towards the specific output you desire. By understanding these building blocks, you'll be able to unlock Gemini's full potential and consistently create impressive results.

Learning Objectives

By the end of this chapter, you will be able to:

- Understand the importance of clarity and specificity in prompt writing.
- Identify the key elements of providing effective context to Gemini.
- Clearly define the desired format, tone, style, and length of Gemini's output in your prompts.
- Effectively use constraints and specific instructions to guide Gemini's responses.
- Construct well-structured prompts that combine clarity, context, desired output specifications, and instructions.

- Feel more confident in your ability to communicate effectively with Gemini to achieve your desired outcomes.

Clarity and Specificity: Being Direct

Imagine asking a friend to "write something about a cat." **What would they write?** It could be a poem, a short story, a factual description, or even just a single sentence. The possibilities are endless! This illustrates why **clarity and specificity** are crucial in prompt writing. The more direct and precise you are with Gemini, the better it can understand your needs and deliver the output you're looking for.

Why is clarity important?

- **Reduces ambiguity:** Vague prompts leave room for interpretation, which might not align with your intentions.
- **Saves time and effort:** Clear prompts lead to more relevant responses from the start, reducing the need for follow-up prompts and revisions.
- **Improves accuracy:** When Gemini understands exactly what you want, it's more likely to provide accurate and helpful information.

How to be specific:

- **Avoid vague words and phrases:** Instead of "write something," try "write a short story," "summarize this article," or "generate a list of ideas."
- **Specify the topic precisely:** Instead of "tell me about history," try "tell me about the causes of the French Revolution" or "explain the significance of the invention of the printing press."

- **Be explicit about what you *don't* want:** If there are specific aspects you want Gemini to avoid, state them clearly. For example, "Explain the concept of photosynthesis without using overly technical jargon."

Real-World Example:

Let's say you want to understand the basics of blockchain technology.

Vague Prompt: "Tell me about blockchain."

This prompt is too broad. Gemini might provide a very high-level overview that doesn't quite meet your needs.

Specific Prompt: "Explain the concept of blockchain technology in simple terms for someone who has no prior knowledge of it. Focus on what it is, how it works, and its main benefits."

This prompt is much clearer and more specific. It tells Gemini:

- **What to explain:** Blockchain technology.
- **The target audience:** Someone with no prior knowledge.
- **The level of detail:** Simple terms.
- **Specific aspects to cover:** What it is, how it works, and its main benefits.

Sample Exercise:

Rewrite the following vague prompts to make them more clear and specific:

1. "Write a poem about nature."
2. "Explain the internet."
3. "Give me some ideas for dinner."

(Think about what kind of poem, what aspects of the internet, and what kind of dinner ideas you're looking for.)

Context is King: Providing Necessary Background

Imagine trying to understand a conversation you just walked into without knowing what was being discussed beforehand. **It would be confusing, right?** Similarly, Gemini often needs **context** to provide the most relevant and helpful responses. Context provides the necessary background information for Gemini to understand the topic, your goals, and the desired perspective.

Why is context important?

- **Helps Gemini understand the scope:** Context clarifies the boundaries of your request.
- **Provides necessary background information:** Gemini can leverage existing knowledge but needs to know what specific area you're interested in.
- **Ensures relevance:** Context helps Gemini tailor its response to your specific situation or needs.

What kind of context should you provide?

- **The topic or subject matter:** Clearly state what you're talking about.
- **Your role or perspective: Are you a student, a teacher, a business owner, or just curious?**
- **The purpose of the request: What do you hope to achieve with Gemini's response?**
- **Any relevant prior information:** If this is a follow-up question or related to a previous interaction, briefly mention it.

Real-World Example:

Let's say you're planning a trip to Italy and want some recommendations.

Prompt without Context: "What are some things to do in Italy?"

This prompt is too general. Italy is a large country with diverse attractions.

Prompt with Context: "I am planning a 10-day trip to Italy in May with my partner. We are interested in historical sites, good food, and beautiful scenery. We will be starting our trip in Rome and ending in Florence. **What are some must-see attractions and activities in these two cities, as well as suggestions for a possible day trip from either city?**"

This prompt provides valuable context:

- **Location:** Italy, specifically Rome and Florence.
- **Duration:** 10 days.
- **Time of year:** May.
- **Travel companions:** With a partner.
- **Interests:** Historical sites, good food, beautiful scenery.
- **Trip structure:** Starting in Rome, ending in Florence, with potential day trips.

With this context, Gemini can provide much more tailored and helpful recommendations.

Sample Exercise:

Add relevant context to the following prompts to improve their effectiveness:

1. "Write an email."
2. "Explain the benefits of exercise."
3. "Suggest some books to read."

(Think about who the email is for, what kind of benefits you're interested in, and what genres of books you enjoy.)

Defining the Desired Output: Format, Tone, Style, Length

Beyond being clear and providing context, you also need to tell Gemini **what kind of output** you're expecting. This includes specifying the format, tone, style, and desired length of the response.

Format: How should the information be presented?

- **Paragraph:** For general explanations or narratives.
- **List (bulleted or numbered):** For presenting items, steps, or features.
- **Table:** For organizing data in rows and columns.
- **Code:** For generating programming code.
- **Recipe:** For providing cooking instructions.
- **Outline:** For structuring information hierarchically.

Tone: What should be the overall feeling or attitude of the response?

- **Formal:** For professional or academic content.
- **Informal:** For casual conversations or friendly advice.
- **Persuasive:** For arguments or calls to action.
- **Neutral:** For objective information.
- **Humorous:** For lighthearted content (use with caution!).
- **Encouraging:** For motivational or supportive messages.

Style: What writing style should Gemini adopt?

- **Descriptive:** Focusing on detailed descriptions and imagery.

- **Analytical:** Examining information critically and logically.
- **Creative:** Using imaginative language and storytelling.
- **Concise:** Being brief and to the point.
- **Technical:** Using specialized vocabulary (use with caution for beginners!).

Length: How long should the response be?

- **Short:** A few sentences or a brief paragraph.
- **Medium:** A few paragraphs or a page.
- **Long:** Several pages or a detailed report.
- **Specify word count:** "Write a summary in approximately 150 words."

Real-World Example:

Let's say you need to explain a complex topic to a child.

Prompt without Output Specifications: "Explain gravity."

Gemini might provide a scientifically accurate but potentially difficult-to-understand explanation.

Prompt with Output Specifications: "Explain the concept of gravity to a 10-year-old using simple language and analogies. Present your explanation in three short paragraphs with an encouraging tone."

This prompt specifies:

- **Format:** Three short paragraphs.
- **Tone:** Encouraging.
- **Style:** Simple language, using analogies.
- **Target audience:** A 10-year-old.

This will help Gemini tailor its explanation to be age-appropriate and engaging.

Sample Exercise:

For each of the following scenarios, specify the desired format, tone, and style for Gemini's output:

1. You need to create a social media post announcing a new product.
2. You want a step-by-step guide on how to bake a cake.
3. You need a formal report summarizing the findings of a research project.

(Think about the target audience and the purpose of each output.)

Constraints and Instructions: Guiding the AI

Finally, you can further refine your prompts by providing specific **constraints** and **instructions**. These act as additional rules and guidelines for Gemini to follow.

Constraints: Tell Gemini what it *shouldn't* do or include.

- "Do not include any personal opinions."
- "Avoid using jargon."
- "Do not mention the competitor's product."
- "Keep the response under 200 words."

Instructions: Give Gemini specific actions to perform or elements to include.

- "Include a bulleted list of the main points."
- "Start with a catchy headline."
- "Use examples to illustrate your points."
- "Cite your sources."
- "Translate the following text into Spanish."

Real-World Example:

Let's say you're asking Gemini to write a blog post.

Prompt without Constraints or Instructions: "Write a blog post about the benefits of mindfulness."

Gemini might write a general blog post that doesn't quite fit your needs.

Prompt with Constraints and Instructions: "Write a blog post about the top 5 benefits of practicing mindfulness for reducing stress. The blog post should have an engaging and informative tone, be approximately 500 words long, and include a call to action at the end encouraging readers to try a simple mindfulness exercise. Do not include any overly technical psychological terms."

This prompt includes:

- **Specific topic:** Top 5 benefits of mindfulness for reducing stress.
- **Desired tone:** Engaging and informative.
- **Desired length:** Approximately 500 words.
- **Specific instructions:** Include a call to action.
- **Constraint:** Do not use overly technical psychological terms.

This level of guidance will help Gemini create a blog post that is more aligned with your specific requirements.

Sample Exercise:

Add relevant constraints and instructions to the following prompts:

1. "Summarize this news article."
2. "Write a short story about a robot."
3. "Generate ideas for a birthday party."

(Think about what limitations you want to impose and what specific elements you want Gemini to include.)

Putting It All Together: An Example of a Great Prompt

Let's combine all the elements we've discussed to create a well-structured prompt:

Scenario: You are a beginner gardener in a cool climate and want to know which vegetables are easy to grow.

Great Prompt:

"I am a beginner gardener living in a cool climate with short summers. I would like a list of 5 easy-to-grow vegetables suitable for my conditions. For each vegetable, please provide a brief description of how to plant and care for it, focusing on the key steps a beginner needs to know. Present the information in a numbered list with a friendly and encouraging tone. Please ensure the vegetables you recommend are known to thrive in cooler temperatures and do not require a very long growing season. Do not include any vegetables that are known to be difficult for beginners."

Breakdown of the Prompt:

- **Clarity and Specificity:** Asks for a "list of 5 easy-to-grow vegetables suitable for my conditions."
- **Context:** "Beginner gardener," "cool climate with short summers."
- **Desired Output (Format):** Numbered list.
- **Desired Output (Tone):** Friendly and encouraging.
- **Desired Output (Style):** Brief description of planting and care, focusing on key steps.
- **Constraints:** Vegetables should thrive in cooler temperatures, not require a long growing season, and not be difficult for beginners.
- **Instructions:** Provide a brief description of planting and care for each vegetable.

This prompt is clear, provides necessary context, specifies the desired output, and includes relevant constraints and instructions. This will significantly increase the chances of Gemini providing a helpful and relevant response.

Sample Exercises

Now it's your turn to practice! Rewrite the following prompts to make them more effective by applying the principles discussed in this chapter:

1. "Tell me about the stock market."
2. "Write a thank you note."
3. "Give me some ideas for a weekend trip."

(Remember to think about clarity, specificity, context, desired output, constraints, and instructions.)

Action Items

1. **Experiment with Gemini:** Take a prompt you've used before and try rewriting it using the techniques you learned in this chapter. See how the output changes.
2. **Analyze successful prompts:** When you receive a particularly good response from Gemini, try to identify which elements of your prompt contributed to its success.
3. **Practice regularly:** The more you practice writing effective prompts, the better you'll become at it. Try using Gemini for different tasks and consciously focus on crafting clear and detailed prompts.

Checklist: The Anatomy of a Great Prompt

Use this checklist to review your prompts before submitting them to Gemini:

- **Clarity and Specificity: Is my request clear and unambiguous? Have I avoided vague language?**
- **Context: Have I provided enough background information for Gemini to understand my needs?**
- **Desired Output (Format):** Have I specified the desired format of the response (e.g., **list, paragraph, table)?**
- **Desired Output (Tone):** Have I indicated the desired tone (e.g., **formal, informal, persuasive)?**
- **Desired Output (Style):** Have I considered the desired writing style (e.g., **descriptive, analytical)?**
- **Desired Output (Length): Have I given an indication of the desired length of the response?**
- **Constraints: Have I specified anything Gemini should** *not* **do or include?**
- **Instructions: Have I given any specific actions for Gemini to perform or elements to include?**

By consistently applying these principles, you'll be well on your way to mastering the art of prompt writing and creating truly exceptional "gems" with Gemini. Congratulations on taking this important step in your AI interaction journey!

Chapter 5: Basic Prospecting Techniques

Welcome to Chapter 5! In the previous chapter, we explored the fundamental building blocks of a great prompt. Now, we're going to start putting those building blocks to work and learn some **basic prospecting techniques**. Think of prospecting as exploring and discovering what Gemini can do for you. Just like a gold prospector searches for valuable nuggets, you'll learn how to use simple prompts to uncover information, generate ideas, and even tap into Gemini's creative potential.

This chapter will introduce you to four fundamental ways to interact with Gemini: asking effective questions, requesting summaries and explanations, generating lists and outlines, and trying out simple creative prompts. These techniques are the foundation for more advanced interactions, and mastering them will significantly enhance your ability to create "gems" with Gemini.

Learning Objectives

By the end of this chapter, you will be able to:

- Formulate clear and effective questions to get specific answers from Gemini.
- Request concise summaries of text or detailed explanations of concepts.
- Generate useful lists of ideas, items, or steps using Gemini.
- Create basic outlines to structure your thoughts or projects with Gemini's help.
- Craft simple creative prompts to generate short poems or descriptive text.
- Feel comfortable using these basic techniques to explore Gemini's capabilities.

Asking Effective Questions

One of the most straightforward ways to interact with Gemini is by asking questions. However, just like talking to another person, the quality of your question directly impacts the quality of the answer you receive. Learning to ask **effective questions** is a crucial skill for getting the information you need from Gemini.

Key Principles for Asking Effective Questions:

- **Be Clear and Concise:** As we learned in Chapter 4, clarity is key. Get straight to the point and avoid ambiguity.
- **Focus on One Question at a Time:** Asking multiple questions in a single prompt can sometimes lead to less focused answers. Break down complex inquiries into individual questions.
- **Use Specific Keywords:** Incorporate relevant keywords to help Gemini understand the topic you're interested in.
- **Specify the Type of Answer You Need (if applicable): Do you want a yes/no answer, a definition, an explanation, or a comparison?**

Real-World Examples:

Let's look at some examples of how to ask effective questions:

Ineffective Question: "Tell me about space." (Too broad)

Effective Question: "What are the main differences between a planet and a star?" (Clear and specific)

Ineffective Question: "Explain this complicated thing." (Lacks specificity)

Effective Question: "Can you explain the concept of a black hole in simple terms?" (Clear, specific, and indicates desired level of complexity)

Ineffective Question: "What are some things about the Eiffel Tower and the Colosseum?" (Asks multiple things at once)

Effective Questions:

- **"What is the height of the Eiffel Tower?"**
- **"When was the Colosseum in Rome built?"**

Sample Exercise:

Rewrite the following ineffective questions to make them more effective for asking Gemini:

1. **"What's good to eat?"**
2. "Explain climate change."
3. "Tell me about famous artists."

(Think about what specific information you're looking for in each case.)

Requesting Summaries and Explanations

Gemini is excellent at processing and understanding large amounts of text and complex concepts. This makes it a powerful tool for **requesting summaries and explanations**. Whether you need to quickly grasp the main points of an article or understand a new idea, Gemini can help.

How to Request Summaries:

- **Provide the Text:** You can paste the text directly into the prompt or provide a link if it's online.

- **Specify the Desired Length (Optional):** You can ask for a summary in a few sentences, a paragraph, or a specific word count.
- **Indicate the Focus (Optional):** If you're interested in specific aspects of the text, mention them in your prompt.

How to Request Explanations:

- **Clearly State the Concept:** Identify the topic you want explained.
- **Specify the Target Audience (Optional):** If you need the explanation tailored for a specific level of understanding (e.g., a child, a beginner, an expert), mention it.
- **Ask for Examples (Optional):** Requesting examples can often make complex concepts easier to grasp.

Real-World Examples:

Requesting a Summary:

Prompt: "Please summarize the following article in three sentences: [Paste the article text here]"

Prompt: "Can you give me the key takeaways from this webpage: [Insert the URL here]"

Requesting an Explanation:

Prompt: "Explain the process of photosynthesis in simple terms for someone with no background in biology."

Prompt: "What is the difference between artificial intelligence and machine learning? Please provide a brief explanation of each."

Sample Exercise:

Write prompts to ask Gemini for the following:

1. A two-sentence summary of a news article you recently read.
2. An explanation of the concept of "supply and demand" in economics, suitable for a beginner.

Generating Lists and Outlines

Need to brainstorm ideas, create a to-do list, or structure a piece of writing? Gemini can be a valuable assistant for **generating lists and outlines**. By providing a clear topic or goal, you can leverage Gemini's ability to quickly generate relevant information in a structured format.

Generating Lists:

- **Specify the Topic:** Clearly state what the list should be about.
- **Indicate the Desired Number of Items (Optional):** If you have a specific number in mind, include it in your prompt.
- **Mention any Specific Criteria (Optional):** If the list needs to adhere to certain criteria (e.g., "list of healthy breakfast options," "list of famous female scientists"), specify them.

Generating Outlines:

- **Provide the Main Topic or Goal: What is the overall subject you want to outline?**
- **Indicate the Desired Level of Detail (Optional): Do you want a high-level outline with main sections, or a more detailed outline with sub-points?**
- **Specify any Key Areas to Include (Optional):** If there are specific aspects you definitely want to cover, mention them.

Real-World Examples:

Generating a List:

Prompt: "Generate a list of 10 popular tourist attractions in Paris."

Prompt: "What are five creative ideas for a child's birthday party?"

Prompt: "Create a bulleted list of the steps involved in planting a tree."

Generating an Outline:

Prompt: "Create a basic outline for a blog post about the benefits of learning a new language."

Prompt: "Generate an outline for a presentation on the history of the internet. Include at least three main sections."

Sample Exercise:

Write prompts to ask Gemini for the following:

1. A list of five potential hobbies you could try.
2. A simple outline for a short essay about the importance of recycling.

Simple Creative Prompts (poems, short descriptions)

While Gemini is a powerful tool for information retrieval and organization, it can also be used for basic creative tasks. You can use simple prompts to generate short **poems** or **descriptive text**. This is a great way to explore Gemini's language capabilities and even spark your own creativity.

Generating Poems:

- **Specify the Topic or Theme: What should the poem be about?**

- **Indicate the Desired Style or Tone (Optional): Do you want a funny poem, a serious one, or something else?** You can even mention specific poetic forms like a haiku.
- **Specify the Length (Optional): How long should the poem be?**

Generating Short Descriptions:

- **Describe the Subject:** Clearly identify what you want Gemini to describe.
- **Specify any Key Features or Aspects to Focus On (Optional): What are the most important things to include in the description?**
- **Indicate the Desired Tone or Style (Optional): Do you want a vivid and imaginative description, or a more factual one?**

Real-World Examples:

Generating a Poem:

Prompt: "Write a short poem about a rainy day."

Prompt: "Generate a haiku about a blooming flower."

Generating a Short Description:

Prompt: "Describe a cozy fireplace on a cold winter evening."

Prompt: "Write a short, vivid description of a bustling city street at night."

Sample Exercise:

Write prompts to ask Gemini for the following:

1. A short poem about your favorite animal.
2. A brief description of a place you enjoy visiting.

Putting It All Together: An Example

Let's see how we can combine these basic prospecting techniques in a single scenario.

Scenario: You're planning a weekend trip to a nearby city and want some ideas.

1. **Asking a Question: "What are some popular attractions in [City Name]?"**
2. **Generating a List:** "Create a list of five highly-rated restaurants in [City Name] that serve Italian food."
3. **Requesting a Short Description:** "Describe the atmosphere of the historic district in [City Name]."
4. **Generating an Outline:** "Create a simple two-day itinerary outline for a weekend trip to [City Name], including sightseeing and dining."

By using a series of simple prompts, you can gather a significant amount of information and even create a basic plan for your trip.

Sample Exercises

Practice using the techniques you've learned in this chapter:

1. Think of a topic you're curious about and formulate three different effective questions to ask Gemini about it.
2. Find a short online article and write a prompt to ask Gemini for a one-paragraph summary.
3. Imagine you're planning a small event. Write a prompt to generate a list of potential themes.
4. You want to write a short story about a mysterious object. Write a prompt to generate a brief outline for your story.

5. Think of a common everyday object and write a prompt to ask Gemini for a short, creative description of it.

Action Items

1. **Experiment with Each Technique:** Dedicate some time to try out each of the four basic prospecting techniques with Gemini. Use different topics and prompts to see the variety of responses you can get.
2. **Combine Techniques:** Try using multiple techniques in sequence, like in the weekend trip example, to achieve a more complex goal.
3. **Refine Your Prompts:** Pay attention to the quality of Gemini's responses and try to understand how your prompts influenced the output. Experiment with different phrasing and levels of detail.

Checklist: Basic Prospecting Techniques

Use this checklist to remind yourself of the basic techniques you've learned:

- **Asking Effective Questions: Am I being clear, specific, and focused on one question at a time?**
- **Requesting Summaries and Explanations: Have I provided the necessary text or clearly stated the concept I want explained? Have I specified the desired length or level of detail?**
- **Generating Lists and Outlines: Have I clearly stated the topic or goal? Have I considered specifying the number of items or level of detail?**
- **Simple Creative Prompts: Have I clearly described the topic or subject for the poem or description? Have I considered specifying the tone or style?**

Congratulations! You've now learned four fundamental techniques for interacting with Gemini. By mastering these basic prospecting skills, you're well-equipped to start exploring the vast potential of AI interaction and uncovering those valuable "gems." In the next chapter, we'll build upon these foundations and explore some slightly more advanced prompting techniques.

Chapter 6: Advanced Prospecting - Refining Your Approach

In the previous chapter, you learned some fundamental techniques for interacting with Gemini. Now, we're going to take your skills to the next level with **advanced prospecting techniques**. These methods will allow you to refine your approach, exert more control over Gemini's output, and unlock even more sophisticated "gems."

Think of this chapter as learning to use more specialized tools in your prospecting toolkit. We'll explore how to guide Gemini through iterative prompting, assign it specific roles, provide examples, encourage reasoning, and even tell it what *not* to do. Mastering these techniques will significantly enhance your ability to get precisely what you need from Gemini.

Learning Objectives

By the end of this chapter, you will be able to:

- Understand and apply the technique of iterative prompting to refine Gemini's responses step-by-step.
- Effectively assign roles or personas to Gemini to tailor its output to specific contexts.
- Utilize few-shot prompting by providing examples to guide Gemini towards the desired results.
- Employ chain-of-thought prompting to encourage Gemini to explain its reasoning process.
- Use negative prompts to specify what you want Gemini to avoid in its responses.
- Combine these advanced techniques to create more sophisticated and effective prompts.
- Feel more confident in your ability to guide Gemini towards highly specific and valuable outputs.

Iterative Prompting: Refining Results Step-by-Step

Sometimes, your initial prompt might not yield the exact result you're looking for. That's perfectly normal! **Iterative prompting** is a powerful technique that involves refining Gemini's output through a series of follow-up prompts. Think of it as having a conversation where you guide Gemini closer to your desired outcome with each interaction.

How Iterative Prompting Works:

1. **Start with a Clear Initial Prompt:** Begin with a well-structured prompt based on the principles you learned in Chapters 4 and 5.
2. **Review Gemini's Response:** Carefully examine the output. **What aspects are good? What could be improved?**
3. **Provide Specific Feedback:** Based on your review, create a new prompt that specifically addresses the areas you want to refine. Be clear about what you want Gemini to change, add, or remove.
4. **Repeat:** Continue this process of reviewing Gemini's responses and providing targeted feedback until you achieve the desired result.

Real-World Example:

Let's say you initially ask Gemini to write a short story about a cat.

Initial Prompt: "Write a short story about a cat."

Gemini's Response: "Once upon a time, there was a fluffy cat named Whiskers. Whiskers loved to nap in sunny spots and chase mice. One day, Whiskers found a ball of yarn and had a great time playing with it. The end."

This is a very basic story. Let's refine it using iterative prompting.

Second Prompt (Refining the Plot): "That's a good start. **Can you make the story a bit more exciting? Perhaps Whiskers encounters a challenge or goes on a small adventure?**"

Gemini's Response: "Once upon a time, there was a fluffy cat named Whiskers. Whiskers loved to nap in sunny spots and chase mice. One sunny afternoon, while exploring the garden, Whiskers spotted a bright red butterfly fluttering just out of reach. Determined to catch it, Whiskers embarked on a thrilling chase through tall grass and around colorful flowers..."

Third Prompt (Adding Detail): "That's better! **Can you add more descriptive details about the garden and Whiskers's pursuit of the butterfly?** Use sensory language to make it more engaging."

Gemini's Response: "Once upon a time, there was a fluffy cat named Whiskers, whose fur was the color of freshly fallen snow. Whiskers loved to nap in sunbeams that warmed the living room floor and stalk the occasional unsuspecting dust bunny. One glorious afternoon, as the air hummed with the buzz of bees, Whiskers ventured into the garden. There, a butterfly with wings the shade of a fiery sunset danced just beyond a patch of vibrant purple lavender. Its erratic flight sparked a thrill in Whiskers's feline heart. With a low crouch and a twitch of his tail, he began his pursuit, his soft paws padding silently through the cool, damp earth..."

As you can see, through a series of prompts, we were able to guide Gemini from a very simple story to a more engaging and descriptive one.

Sample Exercise:

Write an initial prompt asking Gemini to describe your favorite food. Then, write two follow-up prompts to iteratively refine the description, focusing on different aspects like taste, texture, and smell.

Role-Playing: Assigning a Persona to Gemini

Another powerful technique is to **assign a specific role or persona to Gemini**. By telling Gemini to act like a particular type of person or expert, you can influence its tone, style, and the kind of information it provides. This can be incredibly useful for generating content from different perspectives or for simulating conversations.

How to Use Role-Playing:

- **Clearly Define the Role:** In your prompt, explicitly state the role you want Gemini to adopt. Be specific about the characteristics of this role (e.g., "You are a friendly and knowledgeable travel guide").
- **Ask Questions or Make Requests from That Perspective:** Frame your subsequent prompts as if you are interacting with someone in that role.

Real-World Examples:

Example 1: Travel Advice

Prompt: "You are a friendly and knowledgeable local travel guide in Rome. A tourist is asking you for recommendations for must-see historical sites that are not as crowded as the Colosseum or the Vatican. **What would you suggest?**"

Gemini's Response (as a local guide): "Ah, benvenuto a Roma! **You're looking for historical gems away from the biggest crowds, eh?** Excellent choice! While the Colosseum and Vatican are magnificent, there's so much more to discover. I'd highly recommend a visit to the Pantheon – it's an architectural marvel and usually less packed. Also, consider exploring the Roman Forum and Palatine Hill; while popular, the area is vast, so it often feels less overwhelming. For something truly special, check out the Baths of Caracalla – the ruins are impressive, and you can almost imagine the ancient Romans relaxing there. And don't forget the Capitoline Museums, offering stunning views and incredible artifacts!"

Example 2: Explaining a Concept

Prompt: "You are a patient and enthusiastic elementary school teacher. Explain the water cycle to a group of third-grade students."

Gemini's Response (as a teacher): "Hello everyone! Today, we're going to learn about something super important called the water cycle! Imagine water is like a traveler that goes on an amazing journey. First, the sun warms up the water in lakes, rivers, and oceans, and it turns into a gas called water vapor – that's like the water saying, 'I'm going up!' This is called evaporation. Then, as the water vapor goes up into the sky, it gets cold and turns back into tiny little water droplets or ice crystals, forming clouds – that's called condensation. When the clouds get full of water, it falls back down to Earth as rain, snow, sleet, or hail – that's precipitation! And then, the water collects again in lakes, rivers, and oceans, ready to start its journey all over again! **Isn't that cool?**"

Sample Exercise:

Write two prompts asking Gemini for advice on a hobby you're interested in. In the first prompt, tell Gemini to act as an experienced enthusiast of that hobby. In the second prompt, tell Gemini to act as a complete beginner. Compare the responses.

Few-Shot Prompting: Providing Examples

Few-shot prompting is a technique where you provide Gemini with a few examples of the kind of output you're looking for directly within your prompt. This helps Gemini understand the desired format, style, and content more effectively than just giving instructions.

How to Use Few-Shot Prompting:

1. **Clearly State Your Request:** Begin with your main instruction or question.
2. **Provide Examples:** Include one or more examples of the desired output, clearly separated from your main request. You can use formatting like "Example 1:", "Example 2:", etc.
3. **Ask Gemini to Generate More:** After providing the examples, ask Gemini to generate more responses in the same style.

Real-World Example:

Let's say you want Gemini to generate creative names for a new ice cream flavor.

Prompt:

"Here are some examples of creative ice cream flavor names:

Example 1: Midnight Raspberry Swirl Example 2: Caramel Cloud Crunch Example 3: Lavender Honey Dream

Now, generate three more creative names for ice cream flavors."

Gemini's Response:

"Here are three more creative names for ice cream flavors:

1. Pistachio Paradise Bliss
2. Mango Tango Twist
3. Brown Butter Bourbon Pecan"

By providing examples, you showed Gemini the kind of names you were looking for – descriptive, evocative, and appealing.

Sample Exercise:

You want Gemini to write short, positive affirmations. Provide two examples of affirmations in your prompt and then ask Gemini to generate three more.

Chain-of-Thought Prompting: Encouraging Reasoning

Sometimes, you're not just interested in the final answer but also in the **reasoning process** behind it. **Chain-of-thought prompting** is a technique that encourages Gemini to explain its thinking step-by-step before arriving at a conclusion. This can be particularly useful for complex problems or when you want to understand how Gemini arrived at a particular answer.

How to Use Chain-of-Thought Prompting:

- **Phrase Your Prompt to Encourage Reasoning:** Ask Gemini to "explain your reasoning," "walk through your steps," or "think step-by-step."

- **Break Down Complex Problems (Optional):** If you're dealing with a multi-part problem, break it down into smaller steps in your prompt.

Real-World Example:

Prompt: "A bakery sells cookies for $2 each. **If someone buys 5 cookies, what is the total cost?** Explain your reasoning step-by-step."

Gemini's Response:

"Here's the step-by-step reasoning to find the total cost:

1. **Identify the price per cookie:** The problem states that each cookie costs $2.
2. **Identify the number of cookies purchased:** The problem states that someone buys 5 cookies.
3. **Determine the operation needed:** To find the total cost, you need to multiply the price per cookie by the number of cookies.
4. **Perform the multiplication:** $2 (price per cookie) x 5 (number of cookies) = $10.

Therefore, the total cost of 5 cookies is $10."

As you can see, Gemini not only provided the correct answer but also explained the logical steps it took to arrive at that answer.

Sample Exercise:

Ask Gemini a simple math problem that requires more than one step to solve. In your prompt, ask it to explain its reasoning step-by-step.

Negative Prompts: Specifying What Not to Include

Sometimes, it's easier to define what you *don't* want rather than explicitly stating everything you *do* want. **Negative prompts** allow you to tell Gemini what to avoid in its output. This can be a powerful way to refine results and steer Gemini away from undesirable content.

How to Use Negative Prompts:

- **Use Clear and Direct Language:** Explicitly state what you don't want Gemini to include. Phrases like "Do not include," "Avoid mentioning," or "Without using" are effective.
- **Be Specific:** The more specific you are about what to exclude, the better Gemini can understand your constraints.

Real-World Example:

Let's say you want Gemini to write a summary of a historical event, but you don't want it to include any opinions.

Prompt: "Summarize the main events of the French Revolution. Do not include any personal opinions or interpretations."

Gemini's Response (will focus on factual events without subjective commentary): "The French Revolution was a period of radical social and political upheaval in late eighteenth-century France. Triggered by widespread discontent with the monarchy and the existing social order, key events included the storming of the Bastille in 1789, the Reign of Terror, and the eventual rise of Napoleon Bonaparte. The revolution led to the overthrow of the monarchy, the establishment of a republic, and significant changes in French society and government."

Another Example:

Prompt: "Write a short story about a robot visiting a new planet. Avoid using overly technical scientific jargon."

Gemini's Response (will use simpler language and focus on the narrative): "Unit 734 landed softly on the alien world. The sky was a swirling mix of orange and purple, and strange, glowing plants dotted the landscape. As Unit 734 explored, it encountered creatures that resembled giant, furry caterpillars with large, curious eyes. One of them approached cautiously, offering a luminous, blue fruit..."

Sample Exercise:

Write a prompt asking Gemini to generate ideas for a birthday party theme. Include a negative constraint specifying a theme you want it to avoid.

Putting It All Together: Combining Advanced Techniques

The real power of these advanced techniques comes when you start to combine them. For example, you could use iterative prompting with role-playing to refine a character's dialogue in a story. Or you could use few-shot prompting with chain-of-thought prompting to guide Gemini towards a specific type of solution while also understanding its reasoning.

Experiment with different combinations to see how they can help you achieve your desired outcomes.

Sample Exercises

Practice using these advanced techniques:

1. Use iterative prompting to refine a paragraph you generated in a previous chapter, focusing on improving its clarity and flow.
2. Ask Gemini to act as a famous historical figure and answer a question about their life or work.
3. Provide Gemini with two examples of headlines for a news article and then ask it to generate three more headlines in the same style.
4. Ask Gemini to solve a simple logic puzzle and explain its reasoning step-by-step.
5. Write a prompt asking Gemini to generate a list of potential marketing slogans for a new product, but specifically tell it to avoid clichés.

Action Items

1. **Focus on One Technique at a Time:** Spend some time experimenting with each advanced technique individually to fully understand how it works.
2. **Try Combining Techniques:** Once you're comfortable with each technique, start trying to combine two or more in a single prompt or a series of prompts.
3. **Analyze the Results:** Pay close attention to how each technique influences Gemini's output. **What works well for different types of tasks?**
4. **Keep Practicing:** The more you practice using these advanced prompting techniques, the more intuitive they will become.

Checklist: Advanced Prospecting - Refining Your Approach

Use this checklist to review your understanding of the advanced techniques:

- **Iterative Prompting: Am I prepared to refine Gemini's output through a series of targeted prompts?**
- **Role-Playing: Can I effectively assign a persona to Gemini to tailor its responses?**
- **Few-Shot Prompting: Do I understand how to provide examples to guide Gemini's output?**
- **Chain-of-Thought Prompting: Can I phrase my prompts to encourage Gemini to explain its reasoning?**
- **Negative Prompts: Am I able to clearly specify what I want Gemini to avoid in its responses?**

Congratulations on reaching this stage! You've now added some powerful tools to your Gemini interaction toolkit. By mastering these advanced prospecting techniques, you'll be able to achieve even more impressive results and truly unlock the potential of AI-powered content creation. In the next chapter, we'll explore how to apply these skills to specific creative tasks.

Chapter 7: Crafting Brilliant Text

Welcome to Chapter 7! So far, you've learned the fundamentals of prompt writing and explored some basic and advanced techniques for interacting with Gemini. In this chapter, we're going to focus on one of Gemini's most powerful capabilities: **crafting brilliant text**. Whether you need help polishing your writing, generating different types of content, unleashing your creativity, or crafting compelling marketing copy, Gemini can be an invaluable partner.

This chapter will guide you through using Gemini for various text-based tasks. We'll explore how it can assist with writing and editing, generate different forms of text, help you with creative writing endeavors, and even create effective marketing and communication materials. Get ready to discover how Gemini can help you turn your textual ideas into polished "gems."

Learning Objectives

By the end of this chapter, you will be able to:

- Utilize Gemini to assist with grammar, spelling, style, and clarity in your writing.
- Generate different forms of text, including essays, articles, reports, and emails, using effective prompts.
- Leverage Gemini for creative writing projects such as stories, scripts, and poetry.
- Craft compelling marketing and communication copy, including slogans, ad text, and social media posts, with Gemini's help.
- Understand how to tailor your prompts to achieve specific writing goals and styles.
- Feel confident in using Gemini as a powerful tool to enhance your writing abilities and create high-quality text.

Writing and Editing Assistance (Grammar, Style, Clarity)

Even experienced writers can benefit from a fresh pair of eyes to review their work. Gemini can act as your tireless writing assistant, helping you to identify and correct errors in **grammar**, **spelling**, and **punctuation**. Beyond basic corrections, it can also provide valuable feedback on **style** and **clarity**, making your writing more impactful and easier to understand.

How Gemini Can Help:

- **Grammar and Spelling Check:** Simply provide Gemini with your text and ask it to "proofread for grammar and spelling errors."
- **Style Improvement:** You can ask Gemini to "improve the style of this paragraph" or "make this sound more professional/casual/engaging."
- **Clarity Enhancement:** If you think a sentence or paragraph is confusing, ask Gemini to "rephrase this for better clarity" or "explain this in simpler terms."
- **Conciseness:** Gemini can help you eliminate unnecessary words and phrases. Ask it to "make this more concise" or "remove any redundant language."

Real-World Examples:

Example 1: Grammar and Spelling

Your Text: "Their going to the store to by some apples and bananas."

Prompt: "Please proofread the following sentence for grammar and spelling errors: Their going to the store to by some apples and bananas."

Gemini's Response: "The corrected sentence is: They're going to the store to buy some apples and bananas."

Example 2: Style Improvement

Your Text: "The data indicates that there was a significant increase in sales during the last quarter."

Prompt: "Improve the style of the following sentence to make it more direct and impactful: The data indicates that there was a significant increase in sales during the last quarter."

Gemini's Response: "Sales significantly increased last quarter." or "Our sales surged last quarter, according to the data."

Example 3: Clarity Enhancement

Your Text: "The implementation of the aforementioned protocols resulted in a suboptimal outcome due to unforeseen externalities."

Prompt: "Rephrase the following sentence for better clarity and use simpler terms: The implementation of the aforementioned protocols resulted in a suboptimal outcome due to unforeseen externalities."

Gemini's Response: "Following the new procedures led to a worse-than-expected result because of unexpected outside factors."

Sample Exercise:

Take a short piece of your own writing (even a few sentences) and use Gemini to:

1. Check for any grammar or spelling errors.
2. Suggest ways to improve the style.
3. Rephrase a sentence for better clarity.

Generating Different Forms: Essays, Articles, Reports, Emails

Need to write an essay for a class, an article for your blog, a report for work, or a professional email? Gemini can help you generate these different forms of text, saving you time and effort.

How to Guide Gemini:

- **Specify the Type of Text:** Clearly state what you want Gemini to write (e.g., "Write an essay about...", "Generate a report on...", "Draft an email to...").
- **Provide the Topic and Key Information:** Give Gemini all the necessary details it needs to write on the topic.
- **Specify the Purpose and Audience: Who is this text for, and what do you want to achieve with it?**
- **Indicate the Desired Length and Format: Do you need a short email or a multi-page report? Should it be structured with headings and subheadings?**
- **Specify the Tone and Style:** Should it be formal, informal, persuasive, informative, etc.?

Real-World Examples:

Example 1: Generating an Essay

Prompt: "Write a short persuasive essay (approximately 500 words) arguing for the importance of recycling in modern society. The essay should have an introduction, at least three body paragraphs with supporting arguments, and a conclusion. Use a formal and informative tone."

Gemini's Response: (Will generate a structured essay on the topic)

Example 2: Generating an Article

Prompt: "Write a blog article (around 700 words) for beginners explaining the basics of gardening. Include sections on choosing the right plants, preparing the soil, watering, and common beginner mistakes to avoid. Use a friendly and encouraging tone."

Gemini's Response: (Will generate a beginner-friendly article on gardening)

Example 3: Generating a Report

Prompt: "Generate a brief report (about 300 words) summarizing the key findings of a recent marketing campaign. Include data on website traffic, lead generation, and customer engagement. Use a professional and concise tone."

Gemini's Response: (Will generate a summary report based on the provided information)

Example 4: Generating an Email

Prompt: "Draft a polite and professional email to a potential client introducing our company and its services. Briefly mention our experience in the [client's industry] and express interest in scheduling a brief introductory call next week. Use a formal tone."

Gemini's Response: (Will generate a professional introductory email)

Sample Exercise:

Choose one of the following and write a prompt to ask Gemini to generate it:

1. A short email to a friend recommending a new movie.
2. A brief report summarizing the main points of a book you recently read.

3. A short argumentative essay on the benefits of reading fiction.

Creative Writing: Stories, Scripts, Poetry

Unleash your inner storyteller, screenwriter, or poet with Gemini's help! While Gemini might not replace human creativity entirely, it can be a fantastic tool for brainstorming ideas, developing plot points, writing dialogue, or even generating entire pieces of **stories**, **scripts**, or **poetry**.

How to Collaborate with Gemini for Creative Writing:

- **Provide a Premise or Idea:** Start with a basic concept, character, or setting.
- **Specify the Genre and Tone: Do you want a fantasy story, a humorous script, a romantic poem?**
- **Define the Characters (Optional):** Give Gemini details about your characters, their motivations, and their relationships.
- **Outline the Plot (Optional):** If you have a specific plot in mind, you can provide Gemini with an outline to follow.
- **Ask for Specific Elements:** You can ask Gemini to write a scene, a piece of dialogue, a description, or a specific type of poem (e.g., a sonnet, a limerick).
- **Iterate and Refine:** Use iterative prompting (as discussed in Chapter 6) to develop your creative piece further.

Real-World Examples:

Example 1: Writing a Short Story

Prompt: "Write a short science fiction story (around 400 words) about a robot who discovers a hidden garden on a desolate planet. Focus on the robot's emotions and the contrast between the barren landscape and the vibrant garden."

Gemini's Response: (Will generate a science fiction story based on the prompt)

Example 2: Writing a Short Script Scene

Prompt: "Write a short scene for a comedy script. The scene takes place in a crowded elevator. Two characters are trying to have a serious conversation, but they keep getting interrupted by other passengers."

Gemini's Response: (Will generate a script scene with dialogue and actions)

Example 3: Writing a Poem

Prompt: "Write a short, evocative poem about the feeling of nostalgia."

Gemini's Response: (Will generate a poem based on the theme)

Sample Exercise:

Choose one of the following and write a prompt to ask Gemini to generate it:

1. The first paragraph of a fantasy story set in a magical forest.
2. A short dialogue exchange between two characters who have just met.
3. A short poem about the sunrise.

Marketing and Communication Copy

In today's world, effective communication is crucial for businesses and individuals alike. Gemini can be a valuable tool for crafting compelling **marketing and communication copy** that grabs attention and conveys your message effectively.

How Gemini Can Assist with Marketing and Communication:

- **Generating Slogans and Taglines:** Ask Gemini to "generate some catchy slogans for a new coffee shop" or "suggest taglines for a sustainable clothing brand."
- **Writing Ad Copy:** Provide details about your product or service and ask Gemini to "write a short and persuasive ad copy for [product/service] targeting [target audience]."
- **Creating Social Media Posts:** Ask Gemini to "write a engaging social media post (around 150 characters) announcing a new product launch" or "generate a series of tweets about the benefits of [topic]."
- **Drafting Website Content:** You can ask Gemini to "write a short and informative 'About Us' section for a website" or "generate product descriptions for an online store."
- **Crafting Email Marketing Campaigns:** Ask Gemini to "write a compelling subject line and opening paragraph for an email marketing campaign promoting [product/service]."

Real-World Examples:

Example 1: Generating Slogans

Prompt: "Generate three catchy slogans for a new brand of eco-friendly cleaning products."

Gemini's Response: "1. Clean for Today, Green for Tomorrow. 2. Naturally Powerful, Gently Effective. 3. Earth-Friendly Clean, Sparkling Results."

Example 2: Writing Ad Copy

Prompt: "Write a short and persuasive ad copy for a new noise-canceling headphone targeting busy professionals who work from home."

Gemini's Response: "Silence the chaos and boost your focus. Introducing our revolutionary noise-canceling headphones, designed for the ultimate work-from-home experience. Immerse yourself in your tasks and reclaim your concentration. Learn more and order yours today!"

Example 3: Creating a Social Media Post

Prompt: "Write an engaging social media post (under 280 characters) announcing a limited-time discount on our online courses."

Gemini's Response: "Unlock your potential! 🚀 Get 20% off ALL online courses for a limited time. Level up your skills today! #OnlineLearning #Discount #Skills"

Sample Exercise:

Choose one of the following and write a prompt to ask Gemini to generate it:

1. Three potential taglines for a new fitness app.
2. A short social media post announcing a sale at a local bookstore.
3. A brief product description for a new type of ergonomic office chair.

Putting It All Together: Crafting a Blog Post

Let's see how you can use multiple techniques from this chapter to create a complete piece of text, like a blog post.

1. **Initial Prompt (Topic and Tone):** "Write a blog post about the benefits of practicing mindfulness. Use a friendly and informative tone."

2. **Iterative Prompting (Adding Structure):** "That's a good start. **Can you organize the benefits into a numbered list with a brief explanation for each?**"
3. **Role-Playing (Adding Expert Authority):** "Now, act as a mindfulness expert and add a short introductory paragraph explaining what mindfulness is in simple terms."
4. **Negative Prompt (Avoiding Jargon):** "Please review the entire blog post and ensure that you haven't used any overly technical psychological jargon."
5. **Final Prompt (Call to Action):** "Add a concluding paragraph encouraging readers to try a simple mindfulness exercise and suggest one they could try."

By using this combination of techniques, you can guide Gemini to create a well-structured, informative, and engaging blog post on mindfulness.

Sample Exercises

Practice crafting brilliant text with Gemini:

1. Use Gemini to help you edit and improve a piece of writing you've already created.
2. Generate an email to a hypothetical client, introducing a product or service.
3. Write a prompt to ask Gemini to create a short story based on a news headline you recently saw.
4. Generate a few options for a marketing slogan for a local business.

Action Items

1. **Experiment with Different Text Forms:** Try using Gemini to generate various types of text that you might need in your personal or professional life.

2. **Focus on Refinement:** Practice using Gemini to edit and improve existing text, paying attention to grammar, style, and clarity.
3. **Explore Creative Writing:** Don't be afraid to use Gemini as a partner in your creative writing endeavors. See what kind of stories, scripts, or poems you can create together.
4. **Apply to Real-World Scenarios:** Think about situations where you need to write marketing or communication copy and see how Gemini can assist you.

Checklist: Crafting Brilliant Text

Use this checklist to guide your text creation with Gemini:

- **Writing and Editing: Have I considered using Gemini to proofread, improve style, and enhance clarity?**
- **Generating Different Forms: Have I clearly specified the type of text, topic, purpose, audience, length, format, and tone?**
- **Creative Writing: Have I provided a premise, genre, tone, and any necessary details for stories, scripts, or poems?**
- **Marketing and Communication: Have I clearly defined the goal and target audience for slogans, ad copy, social media posts, and website content?**
- **Iteration: Am I prepared to refine the generated text through follow-up prompts?**

Congratulations! You've now learned how to leverage Gemini to craft brilliant text for a wide range of purposes. By mastering these techniques, you'll be able to communicate more effectively, express your creativity, and produce high-quality written content with greater ease and confidence. In the next chapter, we'll delve into using Gemini for research and information gathering.

Chapter 8: Mining for Code

While this book is primarily about interacting with Gemini for text-based tasks, Gemini is also surprisingly helpful when it comes to the world of computer code. Even if you don't have any prior coding experience, understanding how Gemini can assist with code can open up new possibilities and give you a glimpse into the technology that powers much of the digital world.

Think of this chapter as introducing you to a helpful assistant who can speak the language of computers. We'll explore how Gemini can generate simple code snippets, explain what code does, help you find errors, and even translate code from one language to another. While this chapter won't turn you into a programmer overnight, it will equip you with a basic understanding of how Gemini can be a valuable tool in the realm of "mining for code."

Learning Objectives

By the end of this chapter, you will be able to:

- Understand how to ask Gemini to generate basic code snippets in different programming languages.
- Request Gemini to explain what a given piece of code does and understand fundamental coding concepts.
- Utilize Gemini to help identify potential errors or "bugs" in code.
- Ask Gemini to translate simple code snippets from one programming language to another.
- Learn about best practices for using AI as an assistant when working with code.
- Feel more comfortable exploring the world of code with Gemini as a helpful guide.

Generating Code Snippets in Various Languages

One of Gemini's impressive abilities is its capacity to generate code in various programming languages. Whether you need a simple piece of code to automate a task or just want to see how a particular function is written, Gemini can often provide you with a starting point.

How to Ask Gemini to Generate Code:

- **Specify the Programming Language:** Clearly tell Gemini which programming language you need the code in (e.g., Python, JavaScript, Java, C++).
- **Describe the Task Clearly:** Explain exactly what you want the code to do. Be as specific as possible.
- **Indicate Any Specific Requirements (Optional):** If you have any particular constraints or features you want the code to include, mention them.

Real-World Examples:

Example 1: Generating a Simple Python Function

Prompt: "Write a simple Python function that takes two numbers as input and returns their sum."

Gemini's Response:

```
def add_numbers(num1, num2):
  """This function takes two numbers and returns their sum."""
  return num1 + num2

# Example usage:
result = add_numbers(5, 3)
print(result)  # Output: 8
```

Even if you don't know Python, you can see that Gemini has provided a piece of code that seems to define a way to "add_numbers."

Example 2: Generating JavaScript for a Simple Web Task

Prompt: "Generate a short JavaScript code snippet that displays an alert box saying 'Hello!' when a button is clicked."

Gemini's Response:

```
<!DOCTYPE html>
<html>
<head>
<title>Button Alert</title>
</head>
<body>

<button onclick="showAlert()">Click Me</button>

<script>
function showAlert() {
  alert("Hello!");
}
</script>

</body>
</html>
```

This example shows how Gemini can generate code for web development. You can see the basic structure of an HTML page with a button and a piece of JavaScript code.

Example 3: Generating Pseudocode for a Logic Problem

Sometimes, you might just want to understand the logic of a program without worrying about a specific language. You can ask Gemini for **pseudocode**, which is a simplified, human-readable way of describing the steps in an algorithm.

Prompt: "Write pseudocode for an algorithm that checks if a given number is even or odd."

Gemini's Response:

```
FUNCTION is_even_or_odd(number)
  IF number MODULO 2 is equal to 0 THEN
    DISPLAY "The number is even"
  ELSE
    DISPLAY "The number is odd"
  ENDIF
ENDFUNCTION
```

This pseudocode clearly outlines the steps involved in checking if a number is even or odd.

Sample Exercise:

Write prompts to ask Gemini to generate the following:

1. A Python function that multiplies two numbers.
2. JavaScript code that changes the text of an HTML element.
3. Pseudocode for an algorithm that finds the largest number in a list.

Explaining Code and Concepts

If you encounter a piece of code that you don't understand, or if you're curious about a particular coding concept, Gemini can act as your personal code explainer.

How to Ask Gemini to Explain Code:

- **Provide the Code:** Paste the code snippet directly into your prompt.
- **Ask Specific Questions:** Be clear about what you want to understand. You can ask for an overall explanation, the purpose of a specific line of code, or the meaning of a particular keyword.

How to Ask Gemini to Explain Coding Concepts:

- **Clearly State the Concept:** Identify the term or idea you want to understand (e.g., **"What is a loop in programming?"**, "Explain the concept of object-oriented programming").
- **Specify the Level of Detail (Optional):** If you need a beginner-friendly explanation or a more in-depth one, mention it.

Real-World Examples:

Example 1: Explaining a Python Code Snippet

Prompt: "Please explain what the following Python code does: `for i in range(5): print(i)`"

Gemini's Response: "This Python code uses a `for` loop to iterate through a sequence of numbers from 0 up to (but not including) 5. In each iteration of the loop, the current number (`i`) is printed to the console. So, when you run this code, it will print the numbers 0, 1, 2, 3, and 4, each on a new line."

Example 2: Explaining a Coding Concept

Prompt: "Explain the concept of a 'variable' in programming in simple terms."

Gemini's Response: "Imagine a variable as a container or a labeled box in the computer's memory. You can put information (like numbers, text, or other data) into this box, and you can use the label (the variable name) to access and change that information later in your program. For example, you might have a variable named 'age' that stores someone's age as a number."

Sample Exercise:

1. Find a short piece of code online (in any language) and ask Gemini to explain what it does.
2. Ask Gemini to explain a basic coding concept like "function" or "if statement" in simple terms.

Debugging Assistance

Encountering errors or "bugs" in code is a common part of the coding process. While Gemini can't always solve complex debugging issues, it can often help you identify potential problems and suggest solutions for simpler errors.

How to Ask Gemini for Debugging Help:

- **Provide the Code with the Error:** Paste the code snippet that is causing the problem.
- **Describe the Error You're Seeing:** Explain what happens when you run the code or what error message you are getting.
- **Ask for Suggestions:** Clearly ask Gemini for help in identifying the issue and suggesting how to fix it.

Real-World Example:

Prompt: "I'm getting an error in this Python code: `name = "Alice" print("Hello, " + name)` The error says 'TypeError: can only concatenate str (not "int") to str'. **What am I doing wrong?**"

Gemini's Response: "The error message 'TypeError: can only concatenate str (not "int") to str' indicates that you are trying to combine a string (text) with an integer (a whole number) using the + operator. In your code, `name` is correctly assigned a string value "Alice". However, it seems like in the actual code you're running (which you haven't provided fully), you might be trying to add an integer to the string.

To fix this, make sure that both parts you are trying to combine with the + operator are strings. If you need to include a number in your output, you can convert it to a string using the `str()` function.

For example, if you had something like `age = 30` and you wanted to print 'Hello, Alice is 30 years old', you would need to do: `print("Hello, " + name + " is " + str(age) + " years old")`"

While the user's example prompt didn't actually have an integer, Gemini correctly identified the common cause of that specific error message and provided a general solution.

Sample Exercise:

Imagine you have the following Python code and you expect it to print the numbers 1 to 5, but it's not working correctly: `for i in range(6): print(i)`. Ask Gemini for help in identifying the issue. (Hint: The `range(6)` will go from 0 to 5).

Translating Code Between Languages

Sometimes, you might find a useful piece of code written in a programming language you're not familiar with. Gemini can often help you understand the logic by translating it into a language you know better.

How to Ask Gemini to Translate Code:

- **Provide the Code in the Source Language:** Paste the code you want to translate.
- **Specify the Source and Target Languages:** Clearly indicate which language the code is currently in and which language you want it translated to.
- **Ask for the Translation:** Simply ask Gemini to "translate this code from [Source Language] to [Target Language]."

Real-World Example:

Prompt: "Translate the following Python code to JavaScript:
```
def greet(name): return "Hello, " + name"
```

Gemini's Response:

```
function greet(name) {
  return "Hello, " + name;
}
```

In this simple example, Gemini successfully translated the Python function into its JavaScript equivalent.

Important Note: Code translation can become more complex with more intricate code that utilizes language-specific features. In such cases, the translated code might require manual adjustments and review by someone familiar with the target language.

Sample Exercise:

Find a very short code snippet in a language like Java or C++ and ask Gemini to translate it into Python.

Best Practices for AI-Assisted Coding

While Gemini can be a helpful tool for working with code, it's important to use it responsibly and effectively. Here are some best practices to keep in mind:

- **Understand the Code:** Don't just blindly copy and paste code generated by Gemini. Make sure you understand what the code is doing before using it in your projects.
- **Test and Verify:** Always test any code generated or translated by Gemini thoroughly to ensure it works as expected and doesn't introduce any errors.
- **Be Specific in Your Prompts:** The more specific you are about what you need the code to do, the better the results you'll get from Gemini.
- **Use It as a Starting Point:** Think of Gemini as a helpful assistant for generating initial drafts or providing explanations. Complex coding tasks will likely still require human expertise and refinement.
- **Be Aware of Limitations:** Gemini is a powerful tool, but it's not a perfect programmer. It might sometimes generate incorrect or inefficient code. Always use your own judgment and critical thinking.

Putting It All Together: Generating and Understanding a Simple Program

Let's combine some of the techniques we've learned. Suppose you want a simple program that tells you if a number is positive, negative, or zero.

1. **Generating Code:** You could ask Gemini: "Write a simple Python program that takes a number as input and prints whether it's positive, negative, or zero."

2. **Understanding the Code:** Once Gemini provides the code, you can ask it to explain specific parts or the overall logic. **For example, "Can you explain what the if, elif, and else statements do in this code?"**
3. **Testing (Mentally or Actually Running):** You can mentally walk through the code with different inputs to see if it produces the expected output. If you have the ability to run Python code, you can actually test it.

This demonstrates how you can use Gemini not just to generate code but also to help you understand the fundamental concepts behind it.

Sample Exercises

Practice your code mining skills with Gemini:

1. Ask Gemini to generate a short code snippet in a language of your choice that prints the message "Hello, World!". Then, ask it to explain the code.
2. Find a simple piece of code online that you don't understand and ask Gemini to explain its functionality.
3. Imagine you have a piece of code that's giving you an error (make up a simple error). Describe the code and the error to Gemini and ask for suggestions on how to fix it.

Action Items

1. **Explore Code Generation:** Try asking Gemini to generate code for simple tasks in different programming languages.
2. **Practice Code Explanation:** Find code snippets online or in tutorials and use Gemini to help you understand them.

3. **Experiment with Debugging Prompts:** If you encounter a coding error (or even a potential error), try asking Gemini for assistance in identifying the problem.

Checklist: Mining for Code

Use this checklist as a reminder when using Gemini for code-related tasks:

- **Code Generation: Have I clearly specified the programming language and the task I want the code to perform?**
- **Code Explanation: Have I provided the code and asked specific questions about what I want to understand?**
- **Debugging Assistance: Have I provided the code, described the error, and clearly asked for help?**
- **Code Translation: Have I specified the source and target languages for the code I want to translate?**
- **Best Practices: Am I remembering to understand, test, and verify any code provided by Gemini?**

Congratulations! You've now taken your first steps into the world of using AI to assist with code. While this chapter provided a basic introduction, remember that Gemini can be a powerful tool for learning about and working with code, even if you're not planning on becoming a professional programmer. Keep experimenting and exploring!

Chapter 9: Unearthing Insights - Data Analysis and Interpretation

While Gemini isn't a dedicated data analysis tool like specialized software, it possesses a remarkable ability to understand and interpret information, including data. In this chapter, we'll explore how you can leverage Gemini to **unearth insights** from complex information, identify basic patterns, generate initial ideas, and understand technical concepts related to data.

Think of Gemini as a helpful assistant who can look at information with a fresh perspective and help you make sense of it. We'll focus on simple techniques that beginners can use to get a basic understanding of data without needing any prior statistical knowledge. This chapter will show you how Gemini can be a valuable tool for initial data exploration and understanding.

Learning Objectives

By the end of this chapter, you will be able to:

- Utilize Gemini to summarize complex information, including data presented in simple formats.
- Ask Gemini to identify basic patterns and trends within provided datasets.
- Generate potential hypotheses or explanations based on observed patterns in data.
- Request Gemini to explain technical concepts related to data analysis in simple terms.
- Understand the limitations of using a language model for data analysis and interpretation.
- Feel more comfortable using Gemini to get a basic understanding of data and extract initial insights.

Summarizing Complex Information

Often, you might encounter reports, articles, or even raw data that contains a lot of information. Gemini can be a great tool for quickly **summarizing complex information** and helping you identify the key takeaways.

How to Ask Gemini to Summarize Data:

- **Provide the Information Clearly:** Present the data or information in a structured and readable format. This could be a list, a short paragraph describing data, or even a simple table.
- **Ask for a Summary Focusing on Key Points:** Clearly instruct Gemini to summarize the main findings or key pieces of information.
- **Specify the Desired Length (Optional):** You can ask for a summary in a few sentences, a paragraph, or a specific number of bullet points.

Real-World Examples:

Example 1: Summarizing Text with Data

Your Input: "A recent study surveyed 1000 people about their favorite fruit. 45% said apples, 30% preferred bananas, 15% chose oranges, and 10% selected other fruits."

Prompt: "Summarize the key findings of this survey about favorite fruits."

Gemini's Response: "The survey of 1000 people found that apples are the most popular fruit (45%), followed by bananas (30%). Oranges were preferred by 15% of respondents, while the remaining 10% favored other fruits."

Example 2: Summarizing a Simple List of Data

Your Input: "Here are the monthly sales figures for a small online store: January: $1200, February: $1500, March: $1800, April: $1600, May: $2000."

Prompt: "Summarize the trend in monthly sales for this online store over the past five months."

Gemini's Response: "The monthly sales for the online store generally show an upward trend over the past five months, with a slight dip in April before a significant increase in May."

Sample Exercise:

Provide Gemini with the following information: "A company's website traffic for the last week was: Monday: 500, Tuesday: 650, Wednesday: 720, Thursday: 680, Friday: 800, Saturday: 450, Sunday: 400." Ask Gemini to summarize the website traffic pattern for the week.

Identifying Patterns and Trends (with provided data)

When you have a set of data, you might want to identify if there are any **patterns** or **trends** within it. Gemini can help you with this by analyzing the data you provide and pointing out potential relationships or tendencies.

How to Ask Gemini to Identify Patterns and Trends:

* **Present the Data Clearly:** Use a simple format like a list, a table (if not too complex), or a descriptive paragraph.

* **Ask Specific Questions about Patterns or Trends:** Prompt Gemini to look for increases, decreases, peaks, lows, or any other noticeable patterns.

Real-World Examples:

Example 1: Identifying Trends in Sales Data

Your Input:

Month	Sales ($)
June	2500
July	2800
August	3100
September	2900
October	3300

Prompt: "Looking at the sales data above, what trends do you observe?"

Gemini's Response: "I observe a generally increasing trend in sales from June to October, with a slight dip in September before a significant increase in October."

Example 2: Identifying Patterns in Survey Responses

Your Input: "A small survey asked 20 people if they prefer coffee or tea in the morning. 14 people said coffee, and 6 people said tea."

Prompt: "Based on this survey data, what is the main pattern you can identify regarding morning beverage preference?"

Gemini's Response: "The main pattern is that, in this small survey, a significantly higher number of people prefer coffee over tea in the morning."

Important Note: Gemini's ability to identify patterns is based on the data you provide. It's crucial to remember that these are observations based on the given information and might not represent broader trends or be statistically significant.

Sample Exercise:

Provide Gemini with the following data: "The average daily temperature in a city for one week was: Monday: 20°C, Tuesday: 22°C, Wednesday: 25°C, Thursday: 23°C, Friday: 21°C, Saturday: 19°C, Sunday: 20°C." Ask Gemini to identify any patterns or trends in the temperature over the week.

Generating Hypotheses

Once you've identified some patterns or trends in your data, you might want to come up with possible explanations for why those patterns exist. Gemini can help you **generate hypotheses**, which are educated guesses or proposed explanations for an observed phenomenon.

How to Ask Gemini to Generate Hypotheses:

- **Present the Observed Pattern or Trend:** Clearly describe the pattern you've noticed in the data.
- **Ask for Possible Explanations:** Prompt Gemini to suggest reasons or factors that might be contributing to this pattern.

Real-World Examples:

Example 1: Generating Hypotheses for Sales Trends

Your Input: "We observed a general increase in sales for our online store from June to October, with a dip in September."

Prompt: "Based on this sales trend, what are some possible reasons for the overall increase and the dip in September?"

Gemini's Response: "Possible reasons for the overall increase in sales from June to October could include increased marketing efforts during those months, seasonal demand for the products, positive customer reviews leading to more purchases, or successful new product launches. The dip in September could potentially be due to the end of a summer promotion, students returning to school and having less free time for online shopping, or a competitor launching a significant campaign."

Example 2: Generating Hypotheses for Survey Results

Your Input: "A survey showed that a significantly higher number of people prefer coffee over tea in the morning."

Prompt: "What are some possible hypotheses to explain why more people in this survey prefer coffee over tea in the morning?"

Gemini's Response: "Some possible hypotheses could be: Coffee contains caffeine, which is known for its stimulating effects and is often sought after in the morning. The survey might have been conducted in a region where coffee is culturally more prevalent. The sample group might consist of individuals who generally prefer the taste or aroma of coffee. Tea might be perceived as a more relaxing beverage and less associated with the morning rush."

Important Note: The hypotheses generated by Gemini are based on general knowledge and the information you provide. They should be considered as starting points for further investigation and might need to be tested or validated with more rigorous analysis.

Sample Exercise:

Based on the website traffic pattern you analyzed in the previous exercise (higher traffic mid-week, lower on weekends), ask Gemini to generate some possible hypotheses to explain this trend.

Explaining Technical Concepts Simply

When working with data, you might encounter technical terms or concepts that are new to you. Gemini can be a valuable resource for **explaining technical concepts simply** and helping you build your understanding of data analysis.

How to Ask Gemini to Explain Technical Concepts:

- **Clearly State the Term or Concept:** Identify the specific term or idea you want to understand (e.g., **"What is 'correlation' in statistics?"**, "Explain what 'data visualization' means").
- **Ask for a Simple Explanation:** Explicitly request an explanation that is easy for beginners to understand, avoiding jargon.
- **Ask for Examples (Optional):** Requesting examples can often make abstract concepts more concrete.

Real-World Examples:

Example 1: Explaining Correlation

Prompt: "Explain the concept of 'correlation' in statistics in simple terms for someone who is new to data analysis. **Can you provide an example?**"

Gemini's Response: "In simple terms, correlation refers to a relationship or connection between two things. It tells us how much one thing changes when the other thing changes. For example, there might be a positive correlation between the number of hours a student studies and their exam scores – generally, as study hours increase, exam scores tend to increase as well. However, correlation doesn't mean that one thing causes the other; it just means they tend to move together."

Example 2: Explaining Data Visualization

Prompt: "Explain what 'data visualization' means in simple terms."

Gemini's Response: "Data visualization is like turning numbers and information into pictures or charts. Instead of just looking at rows and columns of data, you can use graphs, maps, and other visual tools to see patterns, trends, and relationships more easily. Think of a pie chart showing the percentage of different types of fruits people like – that's a form of data visualization that makes the information much easier to understand at a glance."

Sample Exercise:

Ask Gemini to explain the following data analysis terms in simple terms: "average," "percentage change," and "outlier."

Putting It All Together: Analyzing Customer Reviews

Let's imagine you have a few customer reviews for a product and want to get a basic understanding of customer sentiment.

Your Input:

- Review 1: "Love this product! It's easy to use and works great."
- Review 2: "The product is okay, but the instructions were a bit confusing."
- Review 3: "I am very disappointed with this purchase. It broke after only a week."
- Review 4: "Excellent product and fantastic customer service!"
- Review 5: "It's a decent product for the price."

Prompt 1 (Summarizing): "Summarize the overall sentiment expressed in these customer reviews."

Gemini's Response: "The customer reviews express a mixed sentiment. Some customers are very positive about the product's ease of use, performance, and customer service, while others have experienced issues with the instructions or product durability. One review indicates a neutral sentiment, finding the product decent for its price."

Prompt 2 (Identifying Patterns): "What are some common themes or patterns you can identify in these reviews?"

Gemini's Response: "Common themes include positive feedback about ease of use and performance, a negative comment about confusing instructions, a strong negative experience with the product breaking, and praise for customer service."

Prompt 3 (Generating Hypotheses): "Based on these reviews, what are some potential areas where the product or service could be improved?"

Gemini's Response: "Potential areas for improvement could include making the product instructions clearer and more user-friendly, and addressing the issue of product durability to prevent breakage. The positive feedback on customer service should be maintained and potentially highlighted."

This example shows how you can use Gemini to get a basic understanding of qualitative data like customer reviews.

Sample Exercises

Practice unearthing insights with Gemini:

1. Provide Gemini with a short paragraph from a news article that contains some numerical data. Ask it to summarize the key data points.
2. Create a simple table with some fictional data (e.g., the number of hours someone slept each night for a week). Ask Gemini to identify any patterns in their sleep schedule.
3. Describe a trend you've noticed in something (e.g., the price of a certain product over time). Ask Gemini to generate a few possible reasons for this trend.
4. Ask Gemini to explain a simple data-related concept like "average" or "median" in a way that a child could understand.

Action Items

1. **Find Simple Datasets:** Look for simple datasets online (e.g., weather data for a week, results of a small poll) and try using Gemini to summarize them and identify trends.
2. **Analyze Textual Data:** Try using Gemini to analyze the sentiment or identify themes in a few product reviews or social media comments.
3. **Ask for Explanations:** When you encounter a data-related term you don't understand, ask Gemini to explain it simply.

Checklist: Unearthing Insights - Data Analysis and Interpretation

Use this checklist to guide your basic data exploration with Gemini:

- **Summarizing: Have I presented the data or information clearly and asked for a summary of the key points?**
- **Identifying Patterns: Have I presented the data in a readable format and asked specific questions about trends or patterns?**
- **Generating Hypotheses: Have I described the observed pattern and asked for possible explanations?**
- **Explaining Concepts: Have I clearly stated the technical term and asked for a simple explanation?**
- **Limitations: Am I aware that Gemini's data analysis is basic and not a substitute for dedicated tools?**

Congratulations! You've now learned how to use Gemini to unearth some basic insights from data and complex information. Remember that while Gemini can be a helpful starting point, for more in-depth and rigorous data analysis, specialized tools and techniques are necessary. However, for getting a quick overview and understanding basic patterns, Gemini can be a valuable asset in your "gem" creation process.

Chapter 10: Designing and Brainstorming

Welcome to Chapter 10! By this point in the book, you've become familiar with the art of crafting effective prompts for various tasks. In this chapter, we're going to explore how Gemini can be a powerful partner in the initial stages of any project: **designing and brainstorming**. Whether you're trying to come up with fresh ideas, structure a complex project, understand your target audience, or even visualize a concept, Gemini can offer valuable assistance.

Think of Gemini as your collaborative brainstorming buddy, ready to generate ideas, organize your thoughts, and help you flesh out your initial visions. This chapter will equip you with techniques to use Gemini as a creative catalyst and a structured planning tool.

Learning Objectives

By the end of this chapter, you will be able to:

- Utilize Gemini to generate a wide range of ideas for projects, products, and content.
- Create outlines and structures for your projects and writing with Gemini's assistance.
- Develop basic user personas and scenarios to better understand your target audience using Gemini.
- Describe visual concepts, such as layouts and themes, to Gemini to help solidify your ideas.
- Understand how to use Gemini as a tool to enhance your design and brainstorming processes.
- Feel more confident in your ability to leverage Gemini for creative exploration and structured planning.

Generating Ideas for Projects, Products, Content

Every great creation starts with an idea. Gemini can be an incredible tool for **generating ideas** across various domains, whether you're starting a new project, developing a product, or planning content.

How to Ask Gemini to Generate Ideas:

- **Clearly State Your Need:** Tell Gemini what kind of ideas you're looking for. Be specific about the topic or area you're interested in.
- **Specify Any Constraints or Preferences (Optional):** If you have any limitations or preferences (e.g., "ideas for a low-budget project," "content ideas for social media," "product ideas for teenagers"), include them in your prompt.
- **Ask for a Specific Number of Ideas (Optional):** If you want a certain quantity of ideas, specify it (e.g., "Generate 10 ideas for...").
- **Encourage Variety:** You can ask for a mix of practical and innovative ideas.

Real-World Examples:

Example 1: Generating Project Ideas

Prompt: "I want to start a small side project. Generate five different project ideas that I can work on in my spare time, focusing on areas like technology, writing, or creativity."

Gemini's Response: "Here are five side project ideas for you:

1. **Develop a simple mobile app:** Create a utility app that solves a common problem, like a habit tracker or a recipe organizer.

2. **Start a blog or newsletter:** Share your thoughts and expertise on a topic you're passionate about, like personal finance, photography, or a specific hobby.
3. **Write and self-publish an e-book:** Share a story, guide, or collection of your writings on a platform like Amazon Kindle.
4. **Create and sell digital art or designs:** If you have artistic skills, you could create and sell digital artwork, website templates, or social media graphics.
5. **Build a curated resource website:** Compile a list of helpful links, tools, and information on a specific niche topic."

Example 2: Generating Content Ideas

Prompt: "I run a social media account focused on sustainable living. Generate 10 content ideas for Instagram posts that would engage my audience."

Gemini's Response: "Here are 10 Instagram post ideas for your sustainable living account:

1. Share a DIY tutorial for making your own reusable shopping bags.
2. Highlight a small sustainable swap someone can easily make in their daily routine (e.g., switching to bamboo toothbrushes).
3. Create a visually appealing infographic on the environmental impact of fast fashion.
4. Ask your audience to share their favorite sustainable brands or products in the comments.
5. Post a recipe for a delicious and eco-friendly meal using locally sourced ingredients.
6. Share tips for reducing food waste at home.
7. Create a carousel post showcasing the benefits of composting.
8. Feature a local business or individual who is making a positive impact on sustainability.

9. Share a fact or statistic about climate change in an easily digestible format.
10. Run a poll asking your audience about their biggest sustainability challenges and offer solutions."

Example 3: Generating Product Ideas

Prompt: "Brainstorm three innovative product ideas for the pet market that address a common problem faced by pet owners."

Gemini's Response: "Here are three innovative product ideas for the pet market:

1. **Self-Cleaning Litter Box with Odor Neutralization:** A litter box that automatically scoops waste and uses a natural, pet-safe method to eliminate odors, reducing the hassle for cat owners.
2. **Interactive Puzzle Feeder with Personalized Difficulty Levels:** A smart feeder that dispenses food as the pet solves puzzles, providing mental stimulation and preventing overeating. The difficulty could adjust based on the pet's learning progress.
3. **GPS-Enabled Pet Vest with Health Monitoring:** A comfortable vest that allows owners to track their pet's location in real-time and also monitors vital signs like heart rate and activity levels, providing early warnings of potential health issues."

Sample Exercise:

Think of a topic you're interested in (e.g., gardening, cooking, fitness). Write a prompt asking Gemini to generate five ideas related to that topic for a blog post series.

Creating Outlines and Structures

Once you have some ideas, the next step is often to organize them into a logical structure. Gemini can be a valuable tool for **creating outlines and structures** for your projects, writing, presentations, or any other endeavor that requires organization.

How to Ask Gemini to Create Outlines:

- **Clearly State the Topic or Goal:** Tell Gemini what the outline is for (e.g., "Create an outline for a presentation on...", "Generate a structure for a research paper about...").
- **Specify the Level of Detail (Optional): Do you want a high-level outline with main sections, or a more detailed one with sub-points?**
- **Mention Key Areas to Include (Optional):** If there are specific topics or sections you definitely want to cover, list them in your prompt.
- **Indicate the Desired Format (Optional): Do you prefer a numbered list, bullet points, or a hierarchical structure?**

Real-World Examples:

Example 1: Outlining a Presentation

Prompt: "Create a detailed outline for a 30-minute presentation on the benefits of learning a new language. Include an introduction, at least three main benefits with supporting points, and a conclusion."

Gemini's Response:

I. Introduction (5 minutes)
   A. Hook: Start with an engaging question or statistic about language learning.

B. Briefly introduce the topic: The importance and benefits of learning a new language.

C. Outline the presentation's main points.

II. Cognitive Benefits (10 minutes)

A. Improved memory and cognitive skills.

1. Studies showing the link between language learning and brain plasticity.

2. Examples of how learning a new language can sharpen mental abilities.

B. Enhanced problem-solving and multitasking abilities.

1. Explanation of how navigating different linguistic structures improves these skills.

2. Real-world examples of professionals who benefit from multilingualism.

III. Cultural and Social Benefits (10 minutes)

A. Deeper understanding and appreciation of other cultures.

1. How language opens doors to literature, film, and music from other cultures.

2. Personal anecdotes or examples of cultural exchange facilitated by language skills.

B. Increased opportunities for travel and connection with people from different backgrounds.

1. Practical advantages of speaking the local language when traveling.

2. Building relationships and expanding social circles.

IV. Professional and Career Benefits (3 minutes)

A. Increased job opportunities in a globalized world.

B. Improved communication and collaboration in international teams.

V. Conclusion (2 minutes)

A. Briefly summarize the key benefits of learning a new language.

B. End with an inspiring message or call to action (e.g., encourage audience members to start learning a new language).

Example 2: Structuring a Blog Post

Prompt: "Generate a basic outline for a blog post titled '5 Easy Ways to Start a Meditation Practice'."

Gemini's Response:

I. Introduction
    A. Briefly explain what meditation is and its benefits.
    B. Reassure beginners that it doesn't have to be complicated.

II. Find a Quiet Space and Time
    A. Emphasize the importance of minimizing distractions.
    B. Suggest setting aside a specific time each day.

III. Start with Short Sessions
    A. Recommend beginners start with just 5-10 minutes.
    B. Highlight that consistency is more important than duration.

IV. Focus on Your Breath
    A. Explain how to use the breath as an anchor.
    B. Acknowledge that the mind will wander and that's okay.

V. Explore Guided Meditations
    A. Introduce the concept of guided meditations and their benefits for beginners.
    B. Suggest popular apps or resources.

VI. Conclusion
    A. Reiterate the ease of starting a meditation practice.
    B. Encourage readers to be patient and persistent.

Sample Exercise:

Think about a topic you might want to write about or present. Write a prompt asking Gemini to create a basic outline for it with at least three main sections.

Developing User Personas and Scenarios

If you're designing a product, service, or even content, understanding your target audience is crucial. Gemini can help you develop **user personas** (fictional representations of your ideal users) and **scenarios** (stories about how users might interact with your creation).

How to Ask Gemini to Develop User Personas:

- **Describe Your Target Audience:** Provide details about the demographics, motivations, goals, and pain points of your ideal user.
- **Ask for a Persona:** Specifically ask Gemini to create a user persona based on this information, including a name, age, occupation, and a brief background.

How to Ask Gemini to Develop Scenarios:

- **Describe a Situation or Goal:** Outline a specific situation in which a user might interact with your product or service.
- **Ask for a Scenario:** Prompt Gemini to create a scenario describing how the user would use your creation to achieve their goal.

Real-World Examples:

Example 1: Developing a User Persona

Prompt: "I'm designing a mobile app for people who want to learn a new language. Create a user persona for my ideal user. They are likely in their late 20s or early 30s, busy professionals, motivated by travel and personal growth, and have limited time to dedicate to language learning."

Gemini's Response:

User Persona:

- **Name:** Alex Chen
- **Age:** 32
- **Occupation:** Marketing Manager
- **Background:** Alex is a busy marketing professional who works long hours. They've always wanted to learn Spanish to better connect with colleagues and to be able to travel more confidently in Spanish-speaking countries. Alex has tried language learning apps in the past but found it difficult to stay consistent due to their demanding schedule. Their main goals are to learn practical conversational Spanish and to make progress in short, manageable bursts of time. Their biggest pain point is finding the time and motivation to stick with a language learning routine.

Example 2: Developing a User Scenario

Prompt: "Imagine Alex (our user persona from the previous example) is planning a weekend trip to Barcelona. Describe a scenario of how they might use our language learning app to prepare for their trip."

Gemini's Response: "Scenario: Alex has a free 15-minute break during their lunch hour. They open the language learning app on their phone. Knowing they'll be in Barcelona next weekend, they navigate to the 'Travel Phrases' section. They select the 'Ordering Food' module and practice a few key phrases like 'Me gustaría pedir...' (I would like to order...**) and '¿Cuánto cuesta?' (How much does it cost?**). They then quickly review the 'Greetings and Basic Phrases' module to refresh their memory on 'Hola' and 'Gracias'. Before closing the app, they set a reminder for a 10-minute practice session before bed tonight."

Sample Exercise:

Think about a product or service you use regularly. Describe the typical user of that product/service to Gemini and ask it to create a user persona. Then, describe a common situation where that user might use the product/service and ask Gemini to create a scenario.

Assisting with Visual Concepts (describing layouts, themes)

While Gemini primarily deals with text, it can also be helpful in the early stages of **visual concept development**. By describing your ideas for layouts, themes, or visual elements, you can use Gemini to help clarify your thoughts and even generate descriptive text that you can later use to communicate your vision to designers or artists.

How to Describe Visual Concepts to Gemini:

- **Be Specific with Your Descriptions:** Use detailed language to explain what you have in mind.
- **Focus on Key Elements:** Describe the main components, their arrangement, colors, and overall feeling or atmosphere.

- **Ask for Feedback or Suggestions:** You can ask Gemini if your description makes sense or if it has any suggestions for improvement.

Real-World Examples:

Example 1: Describing a Website Layout

Prompt: "Describe a clean and modern website layout for a small online bookstore. The homepage should have a prominent banner image at the top showcasing new arrivals. Below that, I envision three columns: one for featured books, one for bestsellers, and one for staff recommendations. The navigation bar should be simple and located at the very top. The overall feel should be uncluttered and inviting."

Gemini's Response: "This sounds like a well-organized and user-friendly layout. The prominent banner will immediately draw attention to new arrivals. Using three distinct columns for featured, bestseller, and recommended books provides clear pathways for users to discover different types of books. Placing the navigation bar at the top ensures easy access to other sections of the website. The emphasis on a clean and uncluttered feel will contribute to a positive Browse experience."

Example 2: Describing a Color Theme

Prompt: "Describe a color theme for a children's clothing brand that feels playful and energetic but not overwhelming. I'm thinking of using pastel shades with pops of brighter, contrasting colors."

Gemini's Response: "A pastel base with pops of brighter colors sounds like a great way to achieve a playful and energetic yet balanced feel for a children's clothing brand. Imagine soft shades of baby blue, mint green, and pale yellow as the primary colors, creating a gentle and inviting backdrop. Then, introduce pops of brighter colors like sunny orange, vibrant turquoise, or cheerful magenta as accents in details like buttons, patterns, or small design elements. This approach can create a visually appealing and exciting aesthetic without being too harsh or overwhelming for young eyes."

Sample Exercise:

Think about the layout of a room you'd like to design or a color scheme for a project. Write a detailed description of your vision for Gemini.

Putting It All Together: Planning a Weekend Event

Let's see how you can use multiple techniques from this chapter to plan a small weekend event.

1. **Generating Ideas:** "Brainstorm some fun and engaging ideas for a weekend event for a group of 20-30 friends with diverse interests."
2. **Creating an Outline:** "Create a basic two-day itinerary outline for a weekend retreat focused on relaxation and fun, incorporating some of the ideas we just brainstormed."
3. **Developing a User Persona:** "Describe the typical attendee at this weekend event. Consider their age range, interests, and what they might be looking for in this experience."

4. **Assisting with Visual Concepts:** "Describe a cozy and inviting atmosphere for the accommodation where the event will be held. Focus on the decor and overall ambiance."

By using these techniques, you can leverage Gemini to help you plan and visualize your event from the initial idea to the final touches.

Sample Exercises

Practice your design and brainstorming skills with Gemini:

1. Ask Gemini to generate five ideas for a new mobile game aimed at casual players.
2. Create a basic outline for a short online course teaching a skill you have.
3. Describe the ideal customer for a product you've always wanted to create and ask Gemini to develop a user persona for them.
4. Describe the visual theme you'd like for a personal website to Gemini.

Action Items

1. **Use Gemini for Your Next Brainstorm:** The next time you need to come up with ideas for a project, try using Gemini as your brainstorming partner.
2. **Outline Your Next Writing Project:** Before you start writing your next essay, report, or even a long email, ask Gemini to help you create an outline.
3. **Think About Your Audience:** For any project you're working on, try developing a user persona with Gemini to better understand who you're creating for.
4. **Describe Your Visions:** Practice describing visual ideas to Gemini to help solidify your concepts and potentially communicate them to others.

Checklist: Designing and Brainstorming

Use this checklist to guide your design and brainstorming sessions with Gemini:

- **Idea Generation: Have I clearly stated my need and any constraints or preferences?**
- **Outlining: Have I specified the topic, desired level of detail, and any key areas to include?**
- **User Personas: Have I described my target audience in detail and asked for a persona based on that information?**
- **Scenarios: Have I described a situation and asked for a scenario of how a user might interact with my creation?**
- **Visual Concepts: Have I used specific language to describe layouts, themes, and the overall feeling I'm aiming for?**

Congratulations! You've now explored how Gemini can be a valuable partner in the exciting stages of designing and brainstorming. By using these techniques, you can tap into Gemini's vast knowledge and creative potential to bring your ideas to life. In the final chapter, we'll discuss some important ethical considerations and offer some final tips for mastering the art of AI interaction with Gemini.

Chapter 11: Combining Tools - Gemini in Your Workflow

Welcome to Chapter 11! By now, you've learned a variety of techniques for interacting with Gemini to create valuable outputs. In this chapter, we'll explore how to take your skills even further by **combining Gemini with other software and tools** that you likely already use. We'll also delve into how Gemini can assist with research and even touch upon the exciting concept of automating repetitive tasks.

Think of Gemini as a versatile assistant that can enhance your existing workflow, making you more efficient and creative. This chapter will show you practical ways to integrate Gemini into your daily routines to boost your productivity and help you create even more impressive "gems."

Learning Objectives

By the end of this chapter, you will be able to:

- Understand how to integrate Gemini with common software applications to enhance your workflow.
- Utilize Gemini as a research assistant to gather information and understand complex topics.
- Recognize the importance of fact-checking information obtained from Gemini during research.
- Grasp the conceptual possibilities of using Gemini to automate repetitive tasks.
- Identify opportunities to incorporate Gemini into your existing digital routines.
- Feel more confident in leveraging Gemini as a powerful component of your overall workflow.

Integrating Gemini with other software and tools

One of the most practical ways to use Gemini is by integrating it with the software and tools you already rely on. While direct, built-in integration might evolve over time, the fundamental principle involves using Gemini to enhance your work within these applications. The most common way to do this is through simple copy-pasting.

Examples of Integration:

- **Word Processors (e.g., Google Docs, Microsoft Word):**

    - **Brainstorming and Drafting:** You can use Gemini to brainstorm ideas for a document and then copy the generated text into your word processor as a starting point.
    - **Refining Writing:** After drafting a section, you can copy it into Gemini and ask for suggestions on improving clarity, style, or grammar. Then, paste the refined text back into your document.
    - **Summarizing:** If you have a long document, you can copy sections into Gemini and ask for a concise summary to quickly grasp the key points.
- **Example:** You're writing a report in Google Docs. You're stuck on the introduction. You can open Gemini in another tab, ask it to "Write a brief introduction for a report on the impact of social media on society," copy the generated text, and paste it into your Google Doc as a starting point.

- **Email Clients (e.g., Gmail, Outlook):**

- **Drafting Emails:** If you need help composing an email, you can describe the key points to Gemini and ask it to draft a professional or friendly email. Then, copy and paste the draft into your email client.
- **Summarizing Long Threads:** If you're faced with a lengthy email thread, you can copy the text into Gemini and ask for a summary of the main discussion points.
- **Refining Tone:** If you're unsure about the tone of an email you've written, you can paste it into Gemini and ask for feedback or suggestions on making it sound more polite, direct, or persuasive.

- **Example:** You need to write a thank-you email to a client. You can ask Gemini to "Draft a polite thank-you email to [Client Name] for the productive meeting we had today regarding the [Project Name] project," then copy and paste the generated email into Gmail.

- **Spreadsheets (e.g., Google Sheets, Microsoft Excel):**

  - **Understanding Data:** You can describe a set of data in your spreadsheet to Gemini and ask for insights or potential trends (as discussed in Chapter 9).
  - **Generating Formulas (with Caution):** While more complex formulas might require specialized knowledge, you can ask Gemini for suggestions on basic formulas for calculations or data manipulation. **Remember to always verify the accuracy of any formulas generated by AI.**
  - **Summarizing Findings:** After analyzing data in your spreadsheet, you can describe your findings to Gemini and ask it to generate a concise summary in plain language.

115

- **Example:** You have sales data in a Google Sheet. **You can copy a column of numbers and ask Gemini, "What is the average of these numbers?" or "What is the highest and lowest value in this list?"**

- **Note-taking Apps (e.g., Evernote, OneNote):**

  - **Brainstorming Ideas:** You can use Gemini to brainstorm ideas for a new project or topic directly within your note-taking app by simply switching to Gemini in a browser or another window.
  - **Summarizing Notes:** If you have a long set of notes, you can copy and paste them into Gemini for a quick summary.
  - **Generating Outlines:** Based on your notes, you can ask Gemini to create a structured outline to help you organize your thoughts.
- **Example:** You have a page of handwritten notes in OneNote. You can transcribe the key points and then ask Gemini to "Create a bulleted list of the main topics discussed in these notes."

Key Takeaway: The core principle is to leverage Gemini's ability to process and generate text by using simple copy-paste actions between different applications. This allows you to bring Gemini's power directly into your existing workflow.

Using Gemini for research assistance (fact-checking required!)

Gemini can be a valuable **research assistant**, helping you to gather information, understand complex topics, and explore different perspectives. However, it's absolutely crucial to remember that **all information obtained from Gemini should be fact-checked using reliable sources.**

How Gemini Can Assist with Research:

- **Finding Information:** You can ask Gemini to find information on a specific topic, similar to using a search engine. **For example, "What are the main causes of climate change?"** or "Explain the history of the internet."
- **Summarizing Research Papers or Articles:** If you come across a research paper or a lengthy article, you can provide the text to Gemini and ask for a summary of the key findings or arguments.
- **Explaining Complex Concepts:** If you encounter a technical term or a difficult concept during your research, you can ask Gemini to explain it in simpler terms (as we practiced in Chapter 9).
- **Generating Lists of Resources:** You can ask Gemini for a list of reputable sources on a particular topic, although you should still evaluate the credibility of these sources independently.

The Crucial Importance of Fact-Checking:

Large language models like Gemini are trained on vast amounts of text data from the internet. While this allows them to provide a wide range of information, it also means they can sometimes generate inaccurate, outdated, or even fabricated information. This is often referred to as "hallucination."

Therefore, it is your responsibility to verify any information you obtain from Gemini by cross-referencing it with reliable sources such as:

- Reputable news organizations
- Academic journals and publications
- Government websites
- Established encyclopedias and reference materials
- Expert opinions from trusted sources

Example: You ask Gemini, "What was the capital of France in the 17th century?" Gemini might give you the correct answer (Paris), but it's still a good practice to quickly verify this information with a reliable historical source.

Sample Exercise:

Ask Gemini to provide three interesting facts about the Amazon rainforest. Then, take one of those facts and try to verify it using a reputable online source (like a scientific website or a well-known encyclopedia).

Automating repetitive tasks (conceptual)

The idea of **automating repetitive tasks** is an exciting potential application of AI like Gemini. While setting up complex automation workflows might require more advanced tools and programming skills, it's helpful to understand the conceptual possibilities of how Gemini could contribute.

Conceptual Examples of Automation:

- **Content Creation:** Imagine you regularly need to write short product descriptions for an online store. You could potentially train or prompt Gemini to generate these descriptions based on a template and specific product details, saving you time on manual writing.

- **Summarization:** If you need to summarize multiple articles or reports on a daily basis, you could envision a system where Gemini automatically processes these documents and provides you with concise summaries.
- **Data Extraction and Organization:** Conceptually, you could use Gemini to extract specific information from large amounts of text (like customer feedback or survey responses) and organize it into a structured format, although this would likely require careful prompting and verification.
- **Email Management:** In the future, AI could potentially assist with automating responses to common types of emails based on pre-defined rules or learned patterns.

Important Note for Beginners: Direct automation of complex tasks often requires more advanced tools and integration with other systems. The examples above are meant to illustrate the *potential* of how Gemini's text processing and generation capabilities could be applied to automate repetitive work. As AI technology evolves, we may see more user-friendly tools emerge that make these kinds of automation easier for beginners.

Sample Exercise:

Think of a repetitive task you perform regularly (it could be related to writing, organizing information, or even something else). Describe how you could conceptually use Gemini to help automate or simplify that task.

Putting It All Together: A Day in the Life with Gemini

Let's imagine a scenario where you integrate Gemini into your daily workflow:

1. **Morning:** You're drafting an email to your team about an upcoming project deadline. You use Gemini in a separate window to quickly brainstorm the key points you need to include and then copy-paste them into your email draft.
2. **Mid-day:** You're researching a new topic for a blog post. You use Gemini to find relevant articles and summarize the main arguments. You then fact-check the key information using a reputable online encyclopedia.
3. **Afternoon:** You need to write product descriptions for three new items on your online store. You use a consistent template and ask Gemini to generate the descriptions based on the product features and benefits. You review and edit the generated descriptions before publishing them.

This simple scenario illustrates how Gemini can be a versatile assistant throughout your day, helping with various tasks by combining its capabilities with other tools and workflows.

Sample Exercises

Practice integrating Gemini into your workflow:

1. Choose a document you're currently working on (or a short piece of text). Use Gemini to suggest improvements to the writing and then implement those changes in your document.
2. Pick a topic you're curious about and use Gemini to find three interesting facts. Remember to try and verify those facts using another source.
3. Think of a task you do regularly online (e.g., summarizing news articles, drafting social media posts). Briefly describe how you could use Gemini to make that task more efficient.

Action Items

1. **Identify Your Frequent Tasks:** Think about the software and tools you use most often and the types of tasks you perform regularly.
2. **Experiment with Gemini Integration:** Try using Gemini alongside your favorite applications for tasks like brainstorming, drafting, and summarizing.
3. **Practice Research with Fact-Checking:** The next time you need to research something, use Gemini as a starting point but make sure to always verify the information you find.
4. **Consider Automation Possibilities:** Think about repetitive tasks in your workflow and how Gemini's capabilities could potentially be applied to automate or simplify them in the future.

Checklist: Combining Tools - Gemini in Your Workflow

Use this checklist to guide you in integrating Gemini into your daily routines:

- **Software Integration: Have I explored using Gemini with my word processor, email client, spreadsheets, and note-taking apps?**
- **Research Assistance: Am I using Gemini to gather information and understand complex topics?**
- **Fact-Checking: Am I remembering to always verify information obtained from Gemini using reliable sources?**
- **Automation (Conceptual): Have I thought about how Gemini's capabilities could potentially automate repetitive tasks in my workflow?**

Congratulations! You've now reached the final chapter of "Creating Gems with Gemini." By understanding how to combine Gemini with other tools and integrate it into your workflow, you're well on your way to mastering the art of AI interaction. Remember that continuous experimentation and a critical approach will be key to unlocking the full potential of Gemini in your daily life. Keep exploring, keep creating, and keep polishing those "gems"!

Chapter 12: The Ethics of AI Gem Creation

Welcome to the final chapter of "Creating Gems with Gemini"! Throughout this book, you've learned how to effectively interact with Gemini to produce high-quality outputs. As you become more skilled at this art, it's crucial to consider the **ethical implications** of using AI to create content. This chapter will guide you through some important ethical considerations to ensure you're using Gemini responsibly and thoughtfully.

Think of this chapter as equipping you with a moral compass for your AI interactions. Just like any powerful tool, Gemini should be used with awareness and respect for ethical principles. Understanding these guidelines will help you create "gems" responsibly and contribute positively to the evolving landscape of AI and creativity.

Learning Objectives

By the end of this chapter, you will be able to:

- Understand the concept of plagiarism in the context of AI-generated content and how to ensure originality.
- Recognize potential biases in AI outputs and learn strategies for detection and mitigation.
- Apply principles of responsible use when creating content with Gemini.
- Understand the importance of transparency and disclosure when using AI-generated content.
- Think critically about the ethical implications of using AI for content creation.
- Feel confident in your ability to create "gems" with Gemini in an ethical and responsible manner.

Understanding plagiarism and originality

When using AI to generate text, it's important to understand the concepts of **plagiarism** and **originality**. Plagiarism is presenting someone else's work or ideas as your own, without proper attribution. While Gemini generates new text based on its training data, it's crucial to ensure that the content you ultimately use is original and doesn't infringe on anyone's copyright.

Key Considerations:

- **Gemini Generates, You are Responsible:** Remember that while Gemini creates the initial text, you are the one presenting it. Therefore, the responsibility for ensuring its originality lies with you.
- **AI Learns from Existing Data:** Gemini has been trained on a massive dataset of text and code from the internet. This means its outputs might sometimes contain phrases or ideas that are similar to existing content.
- **Copyright and Intellectual Property:** Just like with human-created content, AI-generated content can potentially raise copyright issues if it too closely replicates existing copyrighted material.

How to Ensure Originality and Avoid Plagiarism:

- **Use Gemini as a Starting Point:** Treat Gemini's output as a foundation that you then build upon with your own ideas, insights, and unique voice.
- **Significantly Modify and Personalize:** Don't just copy and paste Gemini's responses directly. Rewrite, rephrase, and add your own perspective to make the content truly your own.

- **Cite Sources if Necessary:** If Gemini provides information that you know comes from a specific source (even if it doesn't explicitly cite it), it's good practice to cite that source in your final output, especially in academic or professional contexts. You can ask Gemini about the sources it used to inform its response.
- **Use Plagiarism Detection Tools:** If you're concerned about unintentional plagiarism, consider using online plagiarism detection tools to check your final content.
- **Focus on Unique Prompts:** Craft prompts that encourage Gemini to generate novel ideas and perspectives rather than simply summarizing existing information.

Real-World Example:

Let's say you ask Gemini to write a short story about a robot who learns to love. If you simply copy and paste Gemini's story and submit it as your own work for a writing contest, that could be considered plagiarism if the story closely resembles existing copyrighted works or if you present it without acknowledging Gemini's contribution (depending on the contest rules). However, if you take Gemini's initial story, add your own characters, plot twists, and unique writing style, the resulting story is more likely to be considered your original work.

Sample Exercise:

Ask Gemini to write a short paragraph on a historical event. Then, rewrite the paragraph in your own words, adding your own analysis or perspective.

Bias detection and mitigation in outputs

AI models like Gemini are trained on data created by humans, and this data can contain **biases**. These biases can sometimes be reflected in Gemini's outputs, leading to unfair, stereotypical, or discriminatory content. It's important to be aware of this potential and learn how to detect and mitigate bias in the "gems" you create.

Types of Bias to Be Aware Of:

- **Gender Bias:** Stereotyping roles, behaviors, or abilities based on gender.
- **Racial Bias:** Making assumptions or generalizations based on race or ethnicity.
- **Cultural Bias:** Favoring one culture or perspective over others.
- **Socioeconomic Bias:** Making assumptions based on a person's economic or social status.

How to Detect and Mitigate Bias:

- **Critically Evaluate Gemini's Output:** Read Gemini's responses carefully and ask yourself if they contain any stereotypes, unfair assumptions, or language that could be considered biased.
- **Use Diverse and Inclusive Prompts:** Frame your prompts in a way that encourages balanced and inclusive responses. Avoid using language that might reinforce stereotypes.
- **Ask Gemini to Consider Different Perspectives:** If you suspect bias, you can explicitly ask Gemini to consider alternative viewpoints or to provide information that challenges a particular bias. **For example, "Are there any counterarguments to this perspective?" or "How might this be viewed from a different cultural standpoint?"**

- **Refine Your Prompts:** If Gemini's initial response contains bias, try rephrasing your prompt to be more neutral and specific.
- **Cross-Reference Information:** Compare Gemini's output with information from diverse and reliable sources to identify any potential biases.
- **Be Mindful of Word Choice:** Pay attention to the language used in Gemini's responses and make adjustments to ensure it is neutral and respectful.

Real-World Example:

You ask Gemini to "Describe a typical CEO." Gemini might initially provide a description that predominantly features male characteristics or stereotypes associated with certain ethnicities. Recognizing this potential bias, you could then refine your prompt to be more inclusive, such as "Describe the characteristics of a successful CEO, ensuring to consider diversity in gender, ethnicity, and background." This might lead Gemini to provide a more balanced and representative description.

Sample Exercise:

Ask Gemini to describe a "successful doctor" or a "typical engineer." Analyze the response for any potential biases. Then, rephrase your prompt to encourage a more inclusive response.

Responsible use of AI-generated content

Beyond plagiarism and bias, there are broader considerations for the **responsible use of AI-generated content**. This involves thinking about the impact of your creations and ensuring you're using Gemini in a way that is ethical and beneficial.

Principles of Responsible Use:

- **Use AI for Good:** Aim to use Gemini to create content that is informative, helpful, entertaining, or that contributes positively in some way. Avoid using it to generate harmful, misleading, or offensive content.
- **Avoid Spreading Misinformation:** Be cautious about generating and sharing information that could be false or misleading, especially on sensitive topics. Always prioritize accuracy and fact-checking (as discussed earlier).
- **Consider the Impact on Human Creators:** Be mindful of the potential impact of AI-generated content on human artists, writers, and other creators. While Gemini can be a powerful tool, consider how your use of it might affect others.
- **Respect Privacy and Confidentiality:** Avoid using Gemini to generate content that could violate someone's privacy or reveal confidential information.
- **Be Transparent with Your Intentions:** Use Gemini in a way that is honest and transparent. Avoid using AI to impersonate others or to create deceptive content.

Real-World Example:

Using Gemini to generate realistic-looking fake news articles and sharing them online to spread misinformation would be an irresponsible use of AI. However, using Gemini to help you write a creative story, to learn about a new topic, or to brainstorm ideas for a community project would generally be considered responsible uses.

Sample Exercise:

Think about a potential use case for Gemini that could have negative consequences if not handled responsibly. Describe the potential harm and how it could be mitigated.

Transparency and disclosure

In many situations, especially in professional or public contexts, it's important to be **transparent and disclose** when you have used AI to generate content. This helps maintain honesty and allows your audience to understand the origin of the information.

When to Consider Disclosure:

- **Academic Work:** If you're using Gemini to assist with research papers or assignments, check your institution's policies on AI use and disclosure.
- **Professional Content:** If you're creating content for a client or for your work, it's often a good practice to inform them about your use of AI, especially if the content is presented as entirely your own.
- **Publicly Shared Content:** If you're publishing articles, blog posts, or social media content that was significantly generated by AI, consider adding a brief disclosure to inform your audience.

How to Disclose:

- **Simple Statement:** You can include a brief statement such as "This content was generated with the assistance of an AI language model."
- **More Detailed Explanation:** You might provide more detail about how you used Gemini in your creative process.
- **Context Matters:** The level of disclosure might depend on the context and your audience.

Real-World Example:

If you write a blog post that was primarily drafted by Gemini, you might include a sentence at the end of the post saying, "This blog post was created with the assistance of the Gemini AI model." This simple disclosure informs your readers about the role AI played in the content creation process.

Sample Exercise:

Imagine you used Gemini to help you write a cover letter for a job application. **Would you disclose this to the hiring manager? Why or why not? What would be an appropriate way to disclose this information if you chose to do so?**

Putting It All Together: Ethical Considerations in Action

Let's say you're creating a presentation for a school project about the history of the internet. You use Gemini to gather information and generate some initial slides.

- **Plagiarism:** You ensure that you rewrite the information in your own words and cite any specific sources that Gemini might have pointed you towards.
- **Bias:** You critically review the content generated by Gemini to ensure it presents a balanced and inclusive history, considering the contributions of diverse individuals and groups.
- **Responsible Use:** You use the information to educate your audience accurately and avoid presenting any misleading or false information.
- **Transparency:** Depending on your school's guidelines, you might disclose that you used AI as a research and drafting tool in your presentation.

By considering these ethical principles throughout your project, you can ensure that you're using Gemini responsibly and creating a valuable and trustworthy "gem."

Sample Exercises

Reflect on the ethical implications of using AI:

1. Describe a scenario where using AI to generate content could potentially lead to harm or negative consequences.
2. Imagine you found a piece of AI-generated text online that is presented as original work but seems very similar to other sources. **What ethical concerns would this raise for you?**
3. Think about a situation where transparency about using AI to create content would be particularly important. Explain why.

Action Items

1. **Always Consider Originality:** Make it a habit to significantly modify and personalize any content generated by Gemini to ensure it reflects your own understanding and voice.
2. **Be Vigilant for Bias:** Develop a critical eye for potential biases in AI outputs and actively work to mitigate them through careful prompting and review.
3. **Prioritize Responsible Use:** Think about the broader impact of your AI-generated content and strive to use Gemini in a way that is ethical and beneficial.
4. **Practice Transparency:** Consider when and how it's appropriate to disclose your use of AI in your creative process.

Checklist: The Ethics of AI Gem Creation

Use this checklist to guide your ethical considerations when creating with Gemini:

- **Originality: Have I ensured that the content I'm using is original and doesn't constitute plagiarism?**
- **Bias: Have I critically evaluated the output for potential biases and taken steps to mitigate them?**
- **Responsible Use: Am I using Gemini in a way that is ethical, avoids harm, and respects others?**
- **Transparency: Have I considered whether and how I should disclose my use of AI in this context?**

Congratulations on completing "Creating Gems with Gemini - Mastering the Art of AI Interaction"! By understanding the techniques and ethical considerations discussed in this book, you are now well-equipped to harness the power of Gemini to create high-quality outputs responsibly and effectively. Keep experimenting, keep learning, and continue to polish those "gems"!

Chapter 13: Troubleshooting - When the Mine Runs Dry

Welcome to Chapter 13! Throughout this book, you've learned how to effectively prompt Gemini to generate valuable "gems." However, like any tool, sometimes your interactions with Gemini might not yield the results you were hoping for. This chapter is all about **troubleshooting** those situations – what to do when the "mine runs dry" and you're not getting the quality outputs you need.

Think of this chapter as your guide to navigating the occasional bumps in the road when working with AI. It's perfectly normal to encounter generic responses, realize limitations, or feel stuck with your prompts. This chapter will equip you with practical strategies to overcome these challenges and get back to creating brilliant "gems."

Learning Objectives

By the end of this chapter, you will be able to:

- Recognize when Gemini's responses are generic or unhelpful.
- Apply techniques to refine your prompts and get more specific and useful outputs.
- Understand the inherent limitations of AI language models like Gemini.
- Develop strategies for working around these limitations to achieve your goals.
- Identify when your prompts are not working effectively and learn how to adjust them to get better results.
- Feel more confident in your ability to troubleshoot common issues and improve your interactions with Gemini.

Dealing with generic or unhelpful responses

Sometimes, you might ask Gemini a question or give it a prompt, and the response you receive feels **generic** or **unhelpful**. This could manifest as a very broad answer, a statement of the obvious, or simply not addressing your specific needs. Don't get discouraged! This is a common occurrence, and there are several things you can do to guide Gemini towards a more useful response.

Strategies for Getting More Specific Responses:

- **Refine Your Prompt with More Detail:** Often, a generic response indicates that Gemini didn't have enough specific information. Try adding more context, details, and constraints to your prompt.

    - **Instead of:** "Tell me about dogs."
    - **Try:** "Tell me about the characteristics of golden retrievers, including their temperament, exercise needs, and common health issues."
- **Specify the Desired Format or Length:** If you need a specific type of output (like a list, a table, or a step-by-step guide) or a certain length (e.g., a short paragraph, a 500-word essay), clearly state this in your prompt.

    - **Instead of:** "Explain how to bake a cake."
    - **Try:** "Explain how to bake a simple vanilla cake for beginners, providing a step-by-step list of instructions."
- **Ask for Examples:** If you're unsure how to apply a concept or want to see it in action, ask Gemini for examples.

- **Instead of:** "Explain different marketing strategies."
- **Try:** "Explain three different marketing strategies for a small online business and provide a real-world example for each."

- **Role-Playing or Adopting a Persona:** Asking Gemini to adopt a specific role or persona can often lead to more focused and tailored responses.

  - **Instead of:** "Explain the theory of relativity."
  - **Try:** "Explain the theory of relativity as if you were a friendly science teacher explaining it to a high school student."

- **Be More Direct with Your Question:** Sometimes, a vague question will yield a vague answer. Try to be as direct and specific as possible about what you want to know or achieve.

  - **Instead of: "What are your thoughts on the current situation?"**
  - **Try: "What are the key challenges and potential solutions for improving renewable energy adoption in urban areas?"**

Real-World Example:

You prompt Gemini: "Write a story." The response you get is a very short and simple story about a cat. This is generic. To get a more engaging story, you could refine your prompt: "Write a short science fiction story (around 300 words) about a robot who discovers a hidden message on an abandoned spaceship. Focus on the robot's feelings of curiosity and wonder." This more detailed prompt will likely yield a much more specific and interesting story.

Sample Exercise:

You ask Gemini: "Give me some ideas for dinner." The response is a very basic list of common dishes. Rewrite the prompt to get more specific and interesting dinner ideas.

Recognizing and working around limitations

It's important to remember that Gemini, like all AI language models, has **limitations**. Understanding these limitations will help you have more realistic expectations and adapt your approach when necessary.

Common Limitations of AI Language Models:

- **Lack of Real-Time Information:** Gemini's knowledge is based on the data it was trained on, which has a cut-off point. It might not have access to the very latest news or real-time events.
- **Potential for Inaccuracies:** While Gemini strives to provide accurate information, it can sometimes generate incorrect or nonsensical responses. This is why fact-checking (as discussed in Chapter 11) is crucial.
- **Inability to Perform Physical Tasks:** Gemini exists as code and cannot physically interact with the world. It can't cook you dinner or drive you to work.
- **Dependence on Training Data:** Gemini's responses are influenced by the patterns and biases present in its training data (as discussed in Chapter 12).
- **Understanding Nuance and Context:** While Gemini is getting better at understanding context, it might sometimes miss subtle nuances or misunderstand complex instructions.

Strategies for Working Around Limitations:

- **Break Down Complex Tasks:** If you're asking Gemini to do something complicated, try breaking it down into smaller, more manageable steps.
- **Ask for Alternative Approaches:** If Gemini can't directly fulfill your request due to a limitation, ask if there are alternative ways to achieve your goal.
- **Use Gemini in Conjunction with Other Tools:** As discussed in Chapter 11, combining Gemini with other software and resources can help you overcome its limitations. For example, you can use Gemini to generate research questions and then use a search engine to find the most up-to-date information.
- **Fact-Check Important Information:** Always verify critical information from Gemini with reliable sources.
- **Be Patient and Experiment:** Sometimes, finding the right way to phrase your prompt to work around a limitation takes some trial and error. Be patient and don't be afraid to experiment with different approaches.

Real-World Example:

You ask Gemini for the current weather in your specific location. Gemini might tell you it doesn't have access to real-time information. To work around this limitation, you could then ask Gemini for general information about the typical weather patterns for this time of year in your region or use a dedicated weather app or website for the most up-to-date forecast.

Sample Exercise:

Think of a task that Gemini would likely not be able to perform due to its limitations. Describe the task and then suggest a way you could use Gemini in conjunction with another tool or strategy to achieve a similar outcome.

Adjusting prompts when stuck

Sometimes, despite your best efforts, you might find yourself **stuck** – Gemini isn't giving you the kind of responses you need, and you're not sure why. In these situations, it's time to **adjust your prompts**. Think of your prompt as a set of instructions. If the instructions aren't clear or effective, the outcome won't be what you want.

Strategies for Adjusting Your Prompts:

- **Try Different Phrasing:** Sometimes, simply rewording your prompt can make a big difference. Gemini might interpret different phrasings in slightly different ways.
- **Add or Remove Keywords:** Experiment with adding more specific keywords or removing unnecessary ones.
- **Change the Tone or Style of Your Prompt:** Try asking in a different tone (e.g., more formal, more informal, more persuasive).
- **Ask Gemini for Suggestions:** If you're truly stuck, you can even ask Gemini for help on how to improve your prompt! For example, "I'm trying to get Gemini to [your goal], but the responses aren't quite right. **Do you have any suggestions on how I could rephrase my prompt?**"
- **Start Over with a Different Approach:** If you've tried several adjustments and still aren't getting the desired results, it might be helpful to take a step back and try a completely different approach to your prompt.
- **Break Down the Problem:** If you're trying to accomplish a complex task with one prompt, try breaking it down into a series of smaller, more focused prompts.

Real-World Example:

You're trying to get Gemini to write a poem about the feeling of autumn, but the poems it generates are very generic and don't capture the specific mood you're looking for. You could try adjusting your prompt by adding more sensory details: "Write a short poem about the feeling of autumn, focusing on the crisp air, the sound of leaves crunching underfoot, and the warm colors of the changing leaves." You could also try specifying a particular style or tone, such as "Write a melancholic poem about the end of summer and the arrival of autumn."

Sample Exercise:

You want Gemini to give you ideas for a birthday gift for a friend who loves to hike. Your initial prompt is "Gift ideas for a hiker." The responses are very general. Rewrite the prompt in at least two different ways to try and get more specific and helpful suggestions.

Putting It All Together: Troubleshooting a Recipe Request

Let's say you prompt Gemini: "Give me a recipe for pasta." The response is a very basic recipe for spaghetti with tomato sauce. You want something more specific. Here's how you could troubleshoot:

1. **Refine with Detail:** "Give me a recipe for a creamy pasta dish with chicken and broccoli."
2. **Specify Format:** "Provide a step-by-step recipe for creamy chicken and broccoli pasta, including a list of ingredients and clear instructions."
3. **Ask for Specifics: "What are some variations I could try for a creamy chicken and broccoli pasta recipe, such as adding different cheeses or vegetables?"**

By progressively refining your prompt, you can move from a generic response to a much more specific and helpful one.

Sample Exercises

Practice your troubleshooting skills:

1. Ask Gemini a very broad question about a complex topic. Analyze the response. Then, rewrite the question to be more specific and see how the response changes.
2. Think of a task you've tried to accomplish with Gemini that didn't work well. Analyze why you think it failed and write down at least two different ways you could rephrase your prompt to get a better outcome.
3. Imagine Gemini gives you an answer that seems factually incorrect. Describe how you would go about verifying that information.

Action Items

1. **Recognize Unhelpful Responses:** Pay attention to when Gemini's responses are too generic and actively try to refine your prompts for better results.
2. **Acknowledge Limitations:** Be aware of Gemini's inherent limitations and think creatively about how to work around them.
3. **Master Prompt Adjustment:** Don't be afraid to experiment with different phrasings, keywords, and tones when your initial prompts aren't working.
4. **Embrace Iteration:** Remember that interacting with Gemini is often an iterative process. You might need to try several prompts and adjustments to get the "gem" you're looking for.

Congratulations! You've now learned valuable strategies for troubleshooting your interactions with Gemini. Remember that encountering challenges is a normal part of the learning process. By applying the techniques discussed in this chapter, you'll be well-equipped to navigate those moments when the "mine runs dry" and continue to create brilliant "gems" with confidence.

Chapter 14: The Future of Gemini and AI Collaboration

Welcome to the final chapter of "Creating Gems with Gemini"! Throughout this book, you've gained a solid foundation in interacting with AI to produce high-quality outputs. Now, let's take a moment to look ahead at the exciting **future of Gemini and the broader landscape of AI collaboration**. Understanding these emerging trends will not only keep you informed but also empower you to continue mastering the art of AI interaction in the years to come.

Think of this chapter as your glimpse into the crystal ball of AI. While predicting the future with absolute certainty is impossible, we can explore current trajectories and potential developments that will shape how we work with AI like Gemini in the future. This chapter aims to inspire you and equip you with the mindset for lifelong learning in this rapidly evolving field.

Learning Objectives

By the end of this chapter, you will be able to:

- Understand some of the potential emerging capabilities of AI language models like Gemini.
- Discuss the evolving role of AI in both creative endeavors and everyday productivity.
- Recognize the importance of continuous learning to stay updated with advancements in AI.
- Identify resources and strategies for lifelong learning in the field of AI.
- Feel excited and prepared for the future of collaboration with AI.

Emerging capabilities

The field of artificial intelligence is advancing at an incredible pace. What seems like science fiction today might become commonplace tomorrow. While we can't know exactly what the future holds for Gemini, we can look at current trends and anticipate some **emerging capabilities** that could significantly impact how we interact with AI.

Potential Near-Future Developments:

- **Enhanced Understanding of Nuance and Context:** Expect AI models like Gemini to become even better at understanding the subtleties of human language, including sarcasm, humor, and complex instructions. This will lead to more accurate and relevant responses with less need for highly specific prompting.
- **Improved Multimodal Capabilities:** Gemini already shows strong multimodal abilities (understanding and generating text, images, audio, and video). We can anticipate further advancements in this area, allowing for more seamless interaction across different types of content. Imagine Gemini helping you create a presentation by generating both the text and suggesting relevant visuals.
- **More Seamless Integration with Other Tools and Platforms:** We're already seeing basic integration through copy-pasting. The future likely holds more sophisticated and direct integrations of AI into the software and platforms we use daily, making AI assistance a more natural part of our workflow.
- **Increased Personalization and Adaptability:** AI models could become even more personalized, learning your individual preferences, writing style, and knowledge base to provide even more tailored and relevant assistance.

- **Enhanced Reasoning and Problem-Solving:** Future versions of Gemini might exhibit more advanced reasoning capabilities, helping you tackle complex problems, analyze intricate data, and generate more insightful solutions.
- **Better Handling of Long-Form Content and Complex Projects:** We might see AI models that can more effectively manage and contribute to longer and more complex creative projects, such as writing entire books or developing comprehensive business plans, with more coherent and consistent outputs.
- **More Natural and Intuitive Interactions:** The way we interact with AI could become even more conversational and intuitive, perhaps moving beyond text-based prompts to include more natural language commands and even voice interactions.

Real-World Example:

Imagine a future where you can simply tell Gemini, "Help me plan a surprise birthday party for my friend who loves hiking and the color blue," and it will not only generate a guest list and suggest hiking-themed decorations and blue-colored party supplies but also draft invitations and even find local hiking trails suitable for a celebration.

Think About It:

What emerging AI capabilities are you most excited about? How do you think these advancements might change the way you work or create?

The evolving role of AI in creativity and productivity

As AI capabilities continue to evolve, so too will its **role in creativity and productivity**. We've already seen how Gemini can assist with brainstorming, drafting, editing, and research. In the future, this role is likely to become even more significant and integrated.

Potential Shifts in AI's Role:

- **From Assistant to Collaborator:** AI might move beyond being just an assistant to becoming a more active collaborator in creative processes. Imagine co-writing a song with an AI that suggests melodies and harmonies, or co-designing a product with AI that optimizes for both aesthetics and functionality.
- **Democratizing Creativity:** AI tools could make creative endeavors more accessible to everyone, regardless of their prior experience or skill level. Someone who has never written a song before might be able to use AI to bring their musical ideas to life.
- **Boosting Human Productivity:** AI will likely become an even more powerful tool for boosting productivity across various industries and tasks, automating routine work, freeing up human professionals to focus on more strategic and complex challenges.
- **New Forms of Human-AI Co-creation:** We might see the emergence of entirely new forms of creativity that are uniquely enabled by the collaboration between humans and AI, leading to innovative and unexpected outcomes.
- **Emphasis on Human Oversight and Critical Thinking:** Even with more advanced AI, human oversight and critical thinking will remain crucial. We will still need to guide the AI, evaluate its outputs, and ensure that the final results align with our goals and values.

Real-World Example:

Consider the field of graphic design. Today, a designer might use AI to generate initial design concepts or to automate repetitive tasks. In the future, we could see AI tools that deeply understand a client's brand and target audience, collaborating with the designer to create highly effective and visually appealing marketing materials in a fraction of the time.

Think About It:

What are some creative or productive tasks in your own life where you think AI could play a more significant role in the future? What are the potential benefits and challenges of this evolution?

Lifelong learning: Staying updated

The world of AI is constantly changing. New models, features, and applications are being developed all the time. To continue mastering the art of AI interaction and to make the most of tools like Gemini, **lifelong learning** is essential. Staying updated will not only enhance your skills but also help you understand the ethical and societal implications of these advancements.

Strategies for Staying Updated:

- **Follow Reputable Tech News Sources:** Keep an eye on well-respected technology news websites, blogs, and publications that cover AI advancements.
- **Explore Online Courses and Tutorials:** Platforms like Coursera, edX, and YouTube offer a wealth of courses and tutorials on AI and related topics, catering to various skill levels.

- **Engage with AI Communities and Forums:**
  Participate in online communities, forums, and social media groups dedicated to AI. This is a great way to learn from others, ask questions, and stay informed about the latest trends.
- **Experiment with New AI Tools and Features:** Don't be afraid to try out new AI tools and features as they become available. Hands-on experience is one of the best ways to learn.
- **Read Research Papers (Optional):** If you want a deeper understanding of the underlying technology, you can explore research papers published in the field of AI.
- **Attend Webinars and Conferences:** Keep an eye out for webinars and conferences related to AI, where experts often share insights into the latest developments.
- **Be Curious and Open-Minded:** Approach the evolving world of AI with curiosity and an open mind. Be willing to adapt and learn new things as the technology continues to advance.

Real-World Example:

You might start by following a few key tech news websites or subscribing to newsletters that focus on AI. You could then explore a free online course that introduces the basics of machine learning. As you become more comfortable, you might join an online forum where users discuss their experiences with different AI tools.

Action Item:

Identify one or two resources (e.g., a news website, a podcast, an online course) that you can start following to stay updated on the latest developments in AI.

Final Thoughts

Congratulations on reaching the end of "Creating Gems with Gemini"! You've embarked on a journey to understand and master the art of interacting with AI, and you've gained valuable skills that will serve you well in this evolving digital landscape. Remember that your learning doesn't stop here. The world of AI is full of possibilities, and by staying curious, experimenting, and embracing lifelong learning, you'll continue to discover new ways to create incredible "gems" with Gemini and other AI tools.

Thank you for joining us on this journey, and we wish you all the best in your future AI collaborations!

Action Items

1. **Continue Experimenting:** Keep practicing the techniques you've learned in this book and explore new ways to interact with Gemini.
2. **Stay Informed:** Make a commitment to stay updated on the latest advancements in AI by following relevant resources.
3. **Share Your Knowledge:** Consider sharing your experiences and insights with others who are also learning about AI.

Checklist: The Future of Gemini and AI Collaboration

Use this checklist to guide your ongoing journey with AI:

- **Emerging Capabilities: Am I aware of potential future advancements in AI language models?**
- **Evolving Role: Do I understand how AI's role in creativity and productivity might continue to change?**

- **Lifelong Learning: Have I identified resources and strategies for staying updated with AI advancements?**
- **Open Mindset: Am I approaching the future of AI with curiosity and a willingness to learn?**

Thank you for reading "Creating Gems with Gemini - Mastering the Art of AI Interaction"! We hope this book has empowered you to confidently and effectively collaborate with AI. Go forth and create your own brilliant "gems"!

Test Your Knowledge

Chapter 1: Introduction - What are AI Gems?

What is the central goal of "Creating Gems with Gemini"?
A) To teach advanced AI programming techniques.
B) To guide readers in effectively interacting with Gemini to produce high-quality outputs.
C) To explore the theoretical underpinnings of large language models.
D) To compare Gemini with other AI models in detail.
Correct Answer: B)
Explanation: The book's goal, as stated in the context, is to teach readers how to interact effectively with Gemini to generate valuable outputs, referred to as "gems." Options A, C, and D are outside the stated scope for beginners.

Who is the target audience for this book?
A) Experienced AI researchers.
B) Professional software developers.
C) Beginners with little to no prior experience with AI or Gemini.
D) Advanced users of other AI models looking to switch to Gemini.
Correct Answer: C)
Explanation: The context explicitly states that the target audience is beginners who have little to no prior experience with AI or Gemini.

What is the term used in the book to describe high-quality outputs generated through effective interaction with Gemini?
A) Nuggets
B) Jewels
C) Gems
D) Diamonds

Correct Answer: C)

Explanation: The book consistently uses the term "gems" to refer to the desired high-quality outputs produced by interacting with Gemini.

What is the primary focus of "Creating Gems with Gemini"?

A) Understanding the complex architecture of Gemini.

B) Mastering the art of prompt engineering for effective AI interaction.

C) Developing custom AI applications using Gemini's API.

D) Evaluating the ethical implications of AI in general.

Correct Answer: B)

Explanation: The book focuses on teaching readers how to interact effectively with Gemini, which is primarily achieved through the skill of prompt engineering.

What should a reader expect to gain from reading this book?

A) The ability to build their own AI models from scratch.

B) A deep understanding of the mathematical principles behind AI.

C) Confidence in interacting with Gemini to produce valuable results.

D) Certification as a Gemini expert.

Correct Answer: C)

Explanation: The book aims to make readers feel confident in their ability to interact with Gemini and produce high-quality outputs.

What is NOT a primary goal of this book according to the context?

A) To teach effective AI interaction.

B) To produce high-quality outputs with Gemini.

C) To provide a theoretical understanding of AI.

D) To target beginners with no prior experience.

Correct Answer: C)

Explanation: While some understanding of AI is implied, the primary focus is on practical interaction rather than a deep theoretical understanding.

What is the core concept that the book revolves around?
A) The limitations of current AI technology.
B) The power of effective communication with AI.
C) The technical specifications of the Gemini model.
D) The history of artificial intelligence.
Correct Answer: B)
Explanation: The book emphasizes that effective interaction, which involves clear and well-crafted prompts, is key to getting the best results from Gemini.

Chapter 2: Your AI Partner - Understanding Gemini

In simple terms, what is Gemini described as in the context of this book?
A) A complex algorithm for data analysis.
B) A powerful AI model capable of understanding and generating human-like text.
C) A physical robot designed for human interaction.
D) A search engine with advanced filtering capabilities.
Correct Answer: B)
Explanation: Gemini is introduced as an AI model that can understand and generate text similar to humans.

What is the primary mode of interaction with Gemini discussed in this book?
A) Through a visual programming interface.
B) Using spoken voice commands.
C) By providing written prompts and receiving text-based responses.
D) Via direct neural interface.

Correct Answer: C)
Explanation: The book focuses on the interaction through text-based prompts and responses.

What is a key characteristic of Gemini that makes it a versatile tool?
A) Its ability to perform complex mathematical calculations.
B) Its vast knowledge base and ability to understand and generate text on a wide range of topics.
C) Its physical dexterity and ability to manipulate objects.
D) Its capacity for independent thought and decision-making.
Correct Answer: B)
Explanation: Gemini's strength lies in its extensive knowledge and language processing capabilities, making it versatile across various subjects.

What is NOT a primary function of Gemini as described in the book?
A) Understanding user requests expressed in natural language.
B) Generating creative content such as stories and poems.
C) Providing real-time financial market analysis.
D) Answering questions based on its training data.
Correct Answer: C)
Explanation: While Gemini can discuss finance, its primary function isn't real-time market analysis, which requires specialized tools and data.

How should beginners approach interacting with Gemini according to the book?
A) With the expectation of perfect and always accurate answers.
B) As a collaborative partner that requires clear and thoughtful communication.
C) As a tool that can replace human creativity and intelligence.

D) With highly technical and specific programming commands.
Correct Answer: B)
Explanation: The book emphasizes a collaborative approach, highlighting the need for clear communication through effective prompts.

What is the foundation that enables Gemini to understand and respond to your prompts?
A) Its emotional intelligence and ability to empathize with users.
B) The vast amount of text and code data it has been trained on.
C) Direct access to all information on the internet in real-time.
D) A complex network of physical sensors and actuators.
Correct Answer: B)
Explanation: Gemini's capabilities stem from the massive dataset it was trained on, allowing it to recognize patterns and generate relevant responses.

What analogy is used to describe the interaction with Gemini in this chapter?
A) Training a pet.
B) Collaborating with a knowledgeable assistant.
C) Operating a complex machine.
D) Searching through a library.
Correct Answer: B)
Explanation: The chapter likely portrays Gemini as a helpful and knowledgeable assistant that users can collaborate with.

Chapter 3: The Art of Asking - Crafting Effective Prompts

What is the most crucial skill for interacting effectively with Gemini?
A) Advanced programming knowledge.
B) The ability to write clear and effective prompts.
C) A deep understanding of AI algorithms.
D) Access to a high-speed internet connection.
Correct Answer: B)
Explanation: The book emphasizes that crafting effective prompts is the key to getting desired results from Gemini.

What is the first step in crafting an effective prompt?
A) Analyzing Gemini's previous responses.
B) Clearly defining your goal or desired output.
C) Using complex and technical language.
D) Providing a very short and concise instruction.
Correct Answer: B)
Explanation: Before writing a prompt, it's essential to know exactly what you want Gemini to do or generate.

Why is it important to be specific in your prompts?
A) To make Gemini feel more appreciated.
B) To ensure Gemini understands your request accurately and provides a relevant response.
C) Because Gemini charges based on the length of the prompt.
D) To confuse other users who might be looking at your prompts.
Correct Answer: B)
Explanation: Specificity helps Gemini understand your needs and reduces the chances of receiving a generic or irrelevant answer.

What is the benefit of providing context in your prompts?
A) It makes the prompts sound more sophisticated.
B) It helps Gemini understand the background and purpose of your request.
C) It allows you to use shorter and simpler instructions.

D) It prevents Gemini from accessing information outside the provided context.
Correct Answer: B)
Explanation: Context gives Gemini the necessary background information to generate a more informed and relevant response.

What role do constraints play in crafting effective prompts?
A) They limit Gemini's creativity and should be avoided.
B) They help focus Gemini's output and ensure it meets specific requirements.
C) They make the prompts harder for beginners to understand.
D) They are only necessary for very complex tasks.
Correct Answer: B)
Explanation: Constraints help narrow down the possibilities and guide Gemini towards a specific type of output.

What is the value of specifying the desired format in your prompts?
A) It doesn't really affect Gemini's output.
B) It ensures the response is presented in a way that is easy for you to use or understand.
C) It makes the prompt longer and therefore more effective.
D) It is only relevant for code generation prompts.
Correct Answer: B)
Explanation: Specifying the format (e.g., list, table, paragraph) helps Gemini present the information in a usable way.

What is the purpose of using clear and simple language in your prompts?
A) To test Gemini's ability to understand complex vocabulary.
B) To minimize the chances of Gemini misinterpreting your request.
C) To make your prompts sound more authoritative.

D) Because Gemini's processing power is limited.
Correct Answer: B)
Explanation: Clear and simple language reduces ambiguity and makes it easier for Gemini to understand your instructions.

Chapter 4: Polishing Your Gems - Iteration and Refinement

What is the process of iteration in the context of interacting with Gemini?
A) Providing a single, perfect prompt and getting the desired output immediately.
B) Asking the same question multiple times without changing the prompt.
C) Refining your prompts based on Gemini's responses to gradually achieve your desired output.
D) Using increasingly complex and technical language in each subsequent prompt.
Correct Answer: C)
Explanation: Iteration involves a cycle of prompting, receiving a response, evaluating it, and then refining the prompt to get closer to the desired result.

Why is iteration often necessary when working with Gemini?
A) Because Gemini is intentionally designed to be unhelpful on the first try.
B) Because it's hard to perfectly articulate your needs in a single prompt.
C) Because Gemini learns from each interaction and needs multiple prompts to understand.
D) Because the book needs to make the process seem more complex than it is.
Correct Answer: B)

Explanation: It's often difficult to formulate the perfect prompt on the first attempt, so iteration allows for adjustments based on the initial responses.

What should you do if Gemini's initial response is not quite what you were looking for?
A) Assume Gemini is incapable of fulfilling your request and give up.
B) Copy and paste the same prompt again.
C) Analyze the response to identify what went wrong and adjust your prompt accordingly.
D) Blame Gemini for not understanding your needs.
Correct Answer: C)
Explanation: The key to iteration is to learn from each response and use that understanding to refine the next prompt.

What are some ways to refine your prompts during the iteration process?
A) Making them shorter and more vague.
B) Adding more specific details, constraints, or desired formats.
C) Switching to a completely different topic.
D) Using only single-word commands.
Correct Answer: B)
Explanation: Adding more specifics is a common and effective way to guide Gemini towards a better output.

What is the benefit of breaking down a complex task into smaller prompts?
A) It confuses Gemini and makes it harder to get a coherent result.
B) It allows you to focus on one aspect of the task at a time and refine each step individually.
C) It makes the overall process take longer than necessary.
D) It is only useful for creative writing tasks.
Correct Answer: B)

Explanation: Breaking down complex tasks makes them more manageable and allows for targeted refinement at each stage.

What should you consider when evaluating Gemini's responses during the iteration process?
A) Only whether the response perfectly matches your initial expectations.
B) Whether the response is accurate, relevant, and moves you closer to your goal.
C) How quickly Gemini generated the response.
D) Whether the response is similar to what other users have reported.
Correct Answer: B)
Explanation: Evaluation should focus on the quality and relevance of the response in relation to your objective.

What is the ultimate goal of the iteration and refinement process?
A) To make Gemini perfectly understand your thoughts without needing clear prompts.
B) To achieve the high-quality output or "gem" that you initially envisioned.
C) To make the interaction with Gemini take as long as possible.
D) To prove that you are smarter than the AI.
Correct Answer: B)
Explanation: The purpose of iteration is to progressively improve the output until it meets your desired standards.

Chapter 5: Unleashing Creativity - Writing and Storytelling

How can Gemini assist with creative writing and storytelling?

A) By automatically writing entire novels without any human input.
B) By providing ideas, generating drafts, helping with plot development, and offering stylistic suggestions.
C) By only correcting grammar and spelling errors in existing text.
D) By translating stories between different languages.
Correct Answer: B)
Explanation: Gemini can be a versatile tool throughout the creative writing process, from initial ideas to refining the final piece.

What is a good way to use Gemini for brainstorming story ideas?
A) Ask it to rewrite existing famous stories.
B) Provide it with a few keywords or concepts and ask it to generate story prompts or outlines.
C) Ask it to analyze the writing style of famous authors.
D) Use it only to come up with character names.
Correct Answer: B)
Explanation: Providing seed ideas and asking for prompts or outlines is an effective way to kickstart the brainstorming process with Gemini.

How can Gemini help with character development in storytelling?
A) By automatically assigning personality traits and backstories.
B) By suggesting character motivations, flaws, and relationships based on a brief description.
C) By only generating physical descriptions of characters.
D) By translating character dialogues into different languages.
Correct Answer: B)
Explanation: Gemini can assist in fleshing out characters by suggesting key elements that make them believable and engaging.

What is a way to use Gemini to overcome writer's block?
A) Ask it to write the entire story for you.
B) Provide it with your current draft and ask for suggestions on where to go next or for alternative plot points.
C) Ask it to analyze your writing style and tell you what you're doing wrong.
D) Use it to generate random words and try to build a story around them.
Correct Answer: B)
Explanation: Getting feedback and alternative ideas from Gemini can help break through creative blocks.

How can you guide Gemini to write in a specific style or tone?
A) By simply stating the desired style or tone in your prompt (e.g., "Write in a humorous tone," "Write in the style of Edgar Allan Poe").
B) By providing it with examples of the style or tone you want it to emulate.
C) Both A and B.
D) Neither A nor B, Gemini cannot control its writing style.
Correct Answer: C)
Explanation: You can either directly instruct Gemini on the desired style or provide examples for it to learn from.

What is an important step to take when using Gemini to generate creative writing?
A) To publish the output directly without any editing.
B) To treat Gemini's output as a first draft and revise and refine it with your own creative input.
C) To claim that Gemini wrote the entire piece without your involvement.
D) To only use Gemini for generating very short pieces of writing.
Correct Answer: B)
Explanation: Gemini is a tool to assist, and your own creative input is essential for producing truly compelling and original work.

How can Gemini help with editing and refining your creative writing?
A) By automatically rewriting your entire story in a different style.
B) By identifying areas for improvement in clarity, flow, and pacing, and suggesting alternative phrasing.
C) By only checking for spelling and grammar errors.
D) By translating your story into another language and back to see if it improves.
Correct Answer: B)
Explanation: Gemini can act as a helpful editor by providing feedback and suggestions for enhancing your writing.

Chapter 6: Mastering Information - Research and Learning

How can Gemini assist with research and learning?
A) By providing real-time access to all information on the internet.
B) By summarizing complex topics, explaining concepts, and generating lists of resources.
C) By conducting experiments and analyzing data.
D) By providing personal opinions and biases on various subjects.
Correct Answer: B)
Explanation: Gemini is excellent at processing and summarizing information, making it a valuable tool for research and learning.

What is a good way to use Gemini to understand a complex topic?
A) Ask it to write a lengthy research paper on the topic.
B) Ask it to explain the topic in simple terms, as if to a beginner.

C) Ask it to provide highly technical and jargon-filled explanations.

D) Ask it to give you its personal opinion on the topic.

Correct Answer: B)

Explanation: For beginners, asking for simplified explanations is an effective way to grasp complex subjects.

How can Gemini help you find relevant resources for a research project?

A) By providing links to any website it finds, regardless of credibility.

B) By generating lists of potential books, articles, or websites related to your topic (though you should still evaluate their reliability).

C) By giving you the answers directly without needing to consult any external sources.

D) By writing your entire research paper for you, including citations.

Correct Answer: B)

Explanation: Gemini can point you towards potential resources, but it's important to critically evaluate their credibility.

What is an important step to take when using Gemini for research?

A) To blindly trust all the information Gemini provides.

B) To cross-reference the information with reliable sources to ensure accuracy.

C) To assume that Gemini has access to all existing knowledge.

D) To use Gemini only for finding obscure or hard-to-find information.

Correct Answer: B)

Explanation: Fact-checking is crucial when using AI for research due to the potential for inaccuracies.

How can Gemini help you summarize a long article or document?

A) By rewriting the entire text in a different style.
B) By extracting the key points and presenting them in a concise format.
C) By translating the text into another language.
D) By providing a detailed critique of the author's writing style.
Correct Answer: B)
Explanation: Summarization is one of Gemini's strengths, allowing you to quickly grasp the main ideas of lengthy texts.

What is a way to use Gemini to learn new vocabulary or concepts?
A) Ask it to generate random lists of words.
B) Ask it for definitions, explanations, and examples of how to use new words or understand new concepts.
C) Ask it to test your knowledge with difficult quizzes.
D) Use it only to translate words from one language to another.
Correct Answer: B)
Explanation: Gemini can act as a helpful tutor by providing definitions, explanations, and examples to aid in learning.

How can Gemini assist you in understanding different perspectives on a topic?
A) By only presenting one side of an argument.
B) By providing summaries of various viewpoints and arguments related to the topic.
C) By telling you which perspective is the "correct" one.
D) By refusing to discuss controversial topics.
Correct Answer: B)
Explanation: Gemini can help you explore different sides of an issue by summarizing various viewpoints.

Chapter 7: Refining Your Voice - Tone and Style Adjustment

Why might you want to adjust the tone and style of Gemini's output?
A) Because Gemini's default tone is always inappropriate.
B) To better suit the specific audience, context, or purpose of your communication.
C) To make the output sound more like it was written by a robot.
D) Because Gemini doesn't have a consistent writing style.
Correct Answer: B)
Explanation: Tailoring the tone and style ensures the output is effective for its intended purpose and audience.

What is a direct way to instruct Gemini to adopt a specific tone?
A) By providing a lengthy explanation of your desired emotional state.
B) By simply stating the desired tone in your prompt (e.g., "Write in a formal tone," "Write with humor").
C) By asking Gemini to analyze the tone of your prompt and match it.
D) By using only emojis to convey the desired tone.
Correct Answer: B)
Explanation: Directly specifying the tone in your prompt is a straightforward way to guide Gemini's output.

How can you guide Gemini to write in a particular style, such as that of a famous author?
A) By asking it to impersonate the author directly.
B) By providing examples of the author's writing and asking Gemini to emulate their style.
C) By telling Gemini the author's biography.
D) By asking Gemini to analyze the author's handwriting.
Correct Answer: B)

Explanation: Providing examples allows Gemini to learn and mimic the stylistic characteristics of a particular writer.

What are some examples of tones you might ask Gemini to adopt?
A) Happy, sad, angry.
B) Formal, informal, persuasive, humorous, academic.
C) Loud, quiet, fast, slow.
D) Red, blue, green.
Correct Answer: B)
Explanation: Option B lists various writing tones that are relevant to communication.

How can you use Gemini to make your writing sound more professional?
A) By asking it to use more complex and technical jargon.
B) By instructing it to adopt a formal and objective tone, and to use precise language.
C) By asking it to write very long and detailed sentences.
D) By using only acronyms and abbreviations.
Correct Answer: B)
Explanation: A formal tone and precise language are key characteristics of professional writing.

How can you use Gemini to make your writing more engaging for a general audience?
A) By asking it to use highly academic and theoretical language.
B) By instructing it to adopt an informal and approachable tone, use relatable examples, and avoid jargon.
C) By asking it to write in a very serious and somber tone.
D) By using only bullet points and short sentences.
Correct Answer: B)
Explanation: An informal tone, relatable examples, and avoidance of jargon make writing more accessible and engaging for a general audience.

What is an effective way to refine the tone of a piece of writing that Gemini has already generated?
A) Simply copy and paste the text and ask Gemini to "make this sound better."
B) Highlight specific sections and ask Gemini to rewrite them with a different tone, or provide feedback on the overall tone and ask for adjustments.
C) Manually rewrite the entire piece yourself.
D) Ask Gemini to translate it into another language and back to see if the tone changes.
Correct Answer: B)
Explanation: Providing specific instructions or feedback on existing text allows for targeted refinement of the tone.

Chapter 8: Mining for Code

How can you ask Gemini to generate a code snippet in a specific programming language?
A) By simply describing the task you want the code to perform, Gemini will automatically choose the best language.
B) By clearly specifying the programming language in your prompt (e.g., "Write a Python function that...").
C) By providing a code snippet in another language and asking Gemini to translate it.
D) Gemini cannot generate code.
Correct Answer: B)
Explanation: You need to explicitly tell Gemini which programming language you need the code in.

What is a good way to ask Gemini to explain a piece of code that you don't understand?
A) Ask it to rewrite the code in a different language.
B) Paste the code into your prompt and ask specific questions about its functionality or specific lines.

C) Ask it to debug the code even if you don't know what it does.
D) Assume the code is too complex for you to understand.
Correct Answer: B)
Explanation: Providing the code and asking targeted questions is the best way to get explanations from Gemini.

How can Gemini assist with debugging code?
A) It can automatically fix all errors in any code you provide.
B) You can provide Gemini with code that has errors and describe the error message or the problem you're encountering, and ask for suggestions.
C) Gemini cannot help with debugging.
D) You need to provide Gemini with a detailed log of the program's execution.
Correct Answer: B)
Explanation: Gemini can often help identify potential issues and suggest solutions for errors in code.

How can you ask Gemini to translate code from one programming language to another?
A) By simply providing the code, Gemini will automatically detect the language and offer a translation.
B) By clearly specifying the source and target programming languages in your prompt along with the code.
C) Gemini cannot translate code between languages.
D) You need to provide a detailed explanation of the logic behind the code.
Correct Answer: B)
Explanation: You need to tell Gemini both the original language and the language you want the code translated into.

What is an important best practice to follow when using AI to assist with coding?
A) Blindly trust and use any code generated by Gemini without understanding it.

B) Always test and verify any code generated or translated by Gemini to ensure it works correctly.
C) Assume that code generated by AI is always the most efficient and secure.
D) Use AI to generate entire software applications without any human oversight.
Correct Answer: B)
Explanation: It's crucial to test and verify AI-generated code to ensure its functionality and security.

What is pseudocode, and how can Gemini help with it?
A) It's a specific programming language that Gemini excels at.
B) It's a simplified, human-readable way of describing the steps in an algorithm, and you can ask Gemini to generate it for a logic problem.
C) It's a type of code that only computers can understand.
D) Gemini cannot help with pseudocode.
Correct Answer: B)
Explanation: Pseudocode helps in outlining the logic of a program in an understandable format, and Gemini can generate it.

When asking Gemini to explain code, what kind of questions should you ask?
A) Only very general questions like "What does this code do?"
B) Specific questions about the overall functionality, the purpose of certain lines, or the meaning of keywords.
C) Only questions about syntax errors.
D) Questions unrelated to the code itself.
Correct Answer: B)
Explanation: Asking specific questions will help you get targeted explanations from Gemini.

Chapter 9: Unearthing Insights - Data Analysis and Interpretation

While Gemini is not a dedicated data analysis tool, how can it assist with understanding data?
A) By performing complex statistical modeling.
B) By summarizing complex information, identifying basic patterns, and explaining technical concepts simply.
C) By directly connecting to and analyzing large databases.
D) By creating interactive data visualizations.
Correct Answer: B)
Explanation: Gemini can help beginners grasp the basics of data by summarizing, finding simple patterns, and explaining terms.

How can you ask Gemini to summarize a set of data?
A) By providing the data in a clear format (like a list or simple table) and asking for a summary of the key findings or trends.
B) By asking it to perform a full statistical analysis of the data.
C) By providing a link to a large dataset online.
D) Gemini cannot summarize data.
Correct Answer: A)
Explanation: Presenting data clearly and asking for a summary is the way to get Gemini's help in this area.

How can you ask Gemini to identify patterns or trends in provided data?
A) By asking it to predict future values based on the data.
B) By presenting the data in a simple format and asking specific questions about increases, decreases, peaks, or other noticeable patterns.
C) By asking it to create a correlation matrix of the data.
D) Gemini cannot identify patterns in data.
Correct Answer: B)

Explanation: You need to guide Gemini by asking specific questions about potential patterns you're interested in.

What is a hypothesis in the context of data analysis, and how can Gemini help generate them?
A) It's a proven fact derived from data, and Gemini can automatically determine it.
B) It's a proposed explanation for an observed pattern, and you can ask Gemini to suggest potential reasons based on the data.
C) It's a complex statistical formula, and Gemini can calculate it for you.
D) Gemini cannot generate hypotheses.
Correct Answer: B)
Explanation: Gemini can help brainstorm potential explanations for data patterns, which are essentially hypotheses.

How can you use Gemini to understand technical concepts related to data analysis?
A) By asking it to perform the calculations associated with those concepts.
B) By clearly stating the term and asking for a simple, beginner-friendly explanation, often with examples.
C) By asking it to provide a highly technical and academic definition.
D) Gemini cannot explain technical concepts.
Correct Answer: B)
Explanation: Gemini can break down complex data analysis terms into simpler language for beginners.

What is an important limitation to keep in mind when using Gemini for data analysis and interpretation?
A) Gemini can only handle very small datasets.
B) Gemini's analysis is based on the data provided and might not be statistically rigorous or representative of broader trends.

C) Gemini requires you to input data using specific programming commands.
D) Gemini can only analyze numerical data, not text-based information.
Correct Answer: B)
Explanation: Gemini provides a basic overview and should not be relied upon for in-depth statistical analysis.

When asking Gemini to identify trends, what kind of data presentation is most effective for beginners?
A) Complex statistical charts with multiple variables.
B) Simple formats like lists, basic tables, or descriptive paragraphs outlining the data.
C) Raw data dumps without any structure.
D) Data presented in a programming language format.
Correct Answer: B)
Explanation: Beginners benefit most from clear and simple data presentations when using Gemini for basic analysis.

Chapter 10: Designing and Brainstorming

How can Gemini assist with generating ideas for projects, products, or content?
A) By automatically executing projects or creating final products.
B) By providing a range of suggestions based on your topic, constraints, and preferences stated in the prompt.
C) By only suggesting ideas that are already very popular or well-known.
D) Gemini cannot generate creative ideas.
Correct Answer: B)
Explanation: Gemini can be a valuable tool for brainstorming by generating a variety of ideas based on your input.

What is a good way to ask Gemini to create an outline or structure for a project?
A) By simply stating the topic and asking for "an outline."
B) By clearly stating the topic or goal, specifying the desired level of detail, and mentioning any key areas you want included.
C) By providing a very short and vague description of your project.
D) Gemini cannot create outlines.
Correct Answer: B)
Explanation: Providing specific instructions about the topic and desired structure helps Gemini create a useful outline.

What are user personas, and how can Gemini help in developing them?
A) They are fictional representations of your ideal users, and you can ask Gemini to create them based on descriptions of your target audience's demographics, motivations, and goals.
B) They are real people who have used your product or service, and Gemini can automatically collect their data.
C) They are detailed technical specifications for a software application, and Gemini can generate them based on your project idea.
D) Gemini cannot help with developing user personas.
Correct Answer: A)
Explanation: User personas are valuable for understanding your audience, and Gemini can help create them based on your descriptions.

What are user scenarios, and how can Gemini assist in developing them?
A) They are potential problems that users might encounter, and Gemini can automatically solve them.
B) They are stories about how users might interact with your product or service to achieve a specific goal, and you can ask Gemini to create these scenarios based on a user persona and a situation.

C) They are legal documents outlining the terms of use for your product, and Gemini can generate them based on your industry.

D) Gemini cannot help with developing user scenarios.

Correct Answer: B)

Explanation: User scenarios help visualize how your creation will be used, and Gemini can assist in developing these narratives.

How can you use Gemini to assist with visual concepts like layouts or themes?

A) By asking it to directly generate images or visual designs.

B) By describing your ideas for layouts, color schemes, or the overall atmosphere in detail and asking for feedback or further suggestions.

C) By providing it with a single keyword and expecting a comprehensive visual design.

D) Gemini cannot assist with visual concepts.

Correct Answer: B)

Explanation: While Gemini doesn't directly create visuals in this context, it can help you articulate and refine your visual ideas through text-based descriptions.

When brainstorming with Gemini, what is a good approach to get a wide range of ideas?

A) Provide very narrow and restrictive prompts to focus Gemini's creativity.

B) Start with broad prompts and gradually narrow down the focus through iteration based on Gemini's suggestions.

C) Only ask for ideas that are very similar to existing popular concepts.

D) Assume that Gemini's first few ideas are the only ones worth considering.

Correct Answer: B)

Explanation: Starting broad and then refining through iteration allows for exploration of a wider range of possibilities.

What is the benefit of developing user personas and scenarios when designing a product or service?
A) It makes the design process take longer and more complicated.
B) It helps you better understand the needs, motivations, and potential interactions of your target audience, leading to more user-centered designs.
C) It guarantees the success of your product or service.
D) It is only useful for designing software applications.
Correct Answer: B)
Explanation: Understanding your users is crucial for creating products and services that meet their needs effectively.

Chapter 11: Combining Tools - Gemini in Your Workflow

What is the most common way to integrate Gemini with other software and tools discussed in the book?
A) Through complex API integrations requiring programming knowledge.
B) By using simple copy-and-paste actions between Gemini and other applications.
C) By installing special plugins for each software program.
D) Gemini cannot be integrated with other software.
Correct Answer: B)
Explanation: The book focuses on beginner-friendly methods, with copy-pasting being the most accessible.

How can you use Gemini with a word processor like Google Docs or Microsoft Word?
A) Only for checking spelling and grammar.
B) For brainstorming ideas, drafting text, refining writing style, and summarizing content through copy-pasting.
C) Gemini cannot be used with word processors.

D) By using complex macros and scripts.
Correct Answer: B)
Explanation: Gemini can assist with various writing-related tasks within word processors using simple copy-paste.

How can Gemini assist with research, and what crucial step should always be taken?
A) By providing definitive answers to any question without the need for verification.
B) By gathering information, summarizing topics, and explaining concepts, but it's crucial to fact-check all information from Gemini using reliable sources.
C) Gemini cannot be used for research as its information is unreliable.
D) By directly accessing and analyzing scientific databases.
Correct Answer: B)
Explanation: Gemini is a research assistant, but its output needs to be verified for accuracy.

What is the concept of automating repetitive tasks with Gemini discussed in this chapter, and what is a key consideration for beginners?
A) Beginners can immediately set up complex automation workflows using Gemini's built-in features.
B) It involves the conceptual possibility of using Gemini's text processing and generation capabilities to streamline repetitive work, but direct automation often requires more advanced tools and careful verification.
C) Gemini can fully automate any task without any human input or oversight.
D) Automation with AI is only relevant for large corporations.
Correct Answer: B)
Explanation: The chapter introduces the idea of automation conceptually, acknowledging that full implementation might be beyond the scope of beginners.

How could Gemini potentially assist with email management?
A) By automatically deleting all spam emails.
B) By drafting responses to common types of emails or summarizing long email threads, requiring user review and editing.
C) Gemini cannot help with email.
D) By sending emails on your behalf without your knowledge.
Correct Answer: B)
Explanation: Gemini's text generation and summarization skills can be applied to email-related tasks.

When using Gemini for research, why is fact-checking so important?
A) Because Gemini charges you more for inaccurate information.
B) Because AI models like Gemini can sometimes generate inaccurate, outdated, or even fabricated information (hallucinations).
C) Because fact-checking makes your research take longer.
D) Because all information on the internet is unreliable.
Correct Answer: B)
Explanation: The potential for inaccuracies in AI-generated content necessitates careful fact-checking.

What is an example of how Gemini could be used with spreadsheets like Google Sheets or Microsoft Excel?
A) To directly manipulate the numerical data and perform complex calculations without user input.
B) To understand data presented in the spreadsheet, suggest basic formulas, or summarize findings in plain language.
C) Gemini cannot interact with spreadsheets.
D) To automatically create charts and graphs without any prompts.
Correct Answer: B)
Explanation: Gemini can help interpret and understand spreadsheet data through text-based interaction.

Chapter 12: The Ethics of AI Gem Creation

What is plagiarism in the context of AI-generated content?
A) Using AI to generate content that is entirely original and cannot be found anywhere else.
B) Presenting AI-generated content as your own work without proper attribution or if it closely resembles existing copyrighted material.
C) Using AI to check your own writing for accidental similarities to other sources.
D) Claiming that a human wrote content that was actually generated by AI.
Correct Answer: B)
Explanation: Even though AI generates the text, the user is responsible for ensuring it doesn't infringe on copyright and is presented ethically.

Why is it important to be aware of potential biases in AI outputs?
A) Because biased content is always more interesting to read.
B) Because AI models are trained on human-created data, which can contain biases that might lead to unfair, stereotypical, or discriminatory content.
C) Because bias is a necessary component of creativity.
D) Because AI is inherently biased against certain topics.
Correct Answer: B)
Explanation: The training data can influence AI outputs, leading to the reflection of existing societal biases.

What are some strategies for detecting and mitigating bias in Gemini's outputs?
A) Blindly trusting all of Gemini's responses as objective.

B) Critically evaluating the output for stereotypes, using diverse prompts, asking for different perspectives, and cross-referencing information.
C) Assuming that if you don't notice bias, it's not there.
D) Only using AI for topics where bias is unlikely to be an issue.
Correct Answer: B)
Explanation: Active evaluation and prompting techniques are necessary to identify and reduce bias.

What does responsible use of AI-generated content entail?
A) Using AI to generate as much content as possible, regardless of its nature.
B) Aiming to use AI for good, avoiding the spread of misinformation, respecting privacy, and being transparent about intentions.
C) Using AI to impersonate others for entertainment purposes.
D) Avoiding any human oversight of AI-generated content to let the AI be truly creative.
Correct Answer: B)
Explanation: Responsible use involves considering the ethical and societal impact of AI-generated content.

Why is transparency and disclosure important when using AI to generate content, especially in professional or public contexts?
A) To make your work seem more innovative and technologically advanced.
B) To maintain honesty and allow your audience to understand the origin of the information.
C) To avoid any potential copyright issues.
D) Because it is legally required in all situations.
Correct Answer: B)
Explanation: Transparency builds trust and provides context for the content's creation.

What is a good practice to follow regarding originality when using Gemini for writing?
A) Copy and paste Gemini's output directly as your own work.
B) Use Gemini's output as a foundation and significantly modify and personalize it with your own ideas and voice.
C) Claim that Gemini is the sole author of the content.
D) Only use Gemini for generating very short sentences or phrases.
Correct Answer: B)
Explanation: Treating AI output as a starting point and adding your own originality is key to ethical use.

In what situations might disclosing your use of AI be particularly important?
A) Only when you are using AI for personal projects that you don't share with anyone.
B) In academic work, professional content creation, or when publicly sharing information that was significantly generated by AI.
C) Only when you are trying to impress someone with your technological skills.
D) Disclosure is never necessary when using AI.
Correct Answer: B)
Explanation: Transparency is especially important in contexts where the audience needs to understand the source and potential biases of the information.

Chapter 13: Troubleshooting - When the Mine Runs Dry

What should you do if Gemini's response to your prompt is generic or unhelpful?
A) Assume Gemini cannot understand your request and give up.

B) Copy and paste the same prompt again hoping for a different result.
C) Refine your prompt by adding more detail, specifying the format, asking for examples, or trying a different phrasing.
D) Blame the AI for not being intelligent enough.
Correct Answer: C)
Explanation: Refining the prompt with more specific information is the primary strategy for dealing with generic responses.

What is a common limitation of AI language models like Gemini that you should be aware of when troubleshooting?
A) They can perfectly predict future events.
B) They have real-time access to all information on the internet.
C) They might lack real-time information and have the potential for inaccuracies.
D) They can perform physical tasks in the real world.
Correct Answer: C)
Explanation: Understanding these limitations helps you set realistic expectations and adapt your approach.

If you're stuck and Gemini isn't giving you the results you need, what is a good strategy for adjusting your prompts?
A) Make your prompts as short and vague as possible.
B) Try different phrasing, add or remove keywords, change the tone, or even ask Gemini for suggestions on how to improve your prompt.
C) Use increasingly complex and technical language.
D) Stick with the same prompt and try submitting it repeatedly.
Correct Answer: B)
Explanation: Experimenting with different aspects of your prompt is key to overcoming roadblocks.

If you're trying to get Gemini to perform a complex task and it's not working, what approach might be helpful?
A) Try to accomplish the entire task with a single, very long prompt.
B) Break down the complex task into a series of smaller, more focused prompts.
C) Assume that Gemini is not capable of handling complex tasks.
D) Ask Gemini to write a computer program to solve the task instead.
Correct Answer: B)
Explanation: Breaking down complex tasks into smaller steps makes them more manageable for Gemini.

When dealing with generic responses, what is the benefit of specifying the desired format in your prompt?
A) It doesn't usually make a difference.
B) It helps Gemini structure the information in a way that is more useful for you (e.g., a list, a table).
C) It makes the prompt harder for Gemini to understand.
D) It is only relevant for code generation.
Correct Answer: B)
Explanation: Specifying the format guides Gemini to present the output in a more structured and usable way.

What should you do if you suspect that the information Gemini has provided is inaccurate?
A) Assume that Gemini is always correct because it's a powerful AI.
B) Immediately share the information as fact without any further verification.
C) Cross-reference the information with reliable sources to confirm its accuracy.
D) Blame Gemini for providing false information.
Correct Answer: C)
Explanation: Fact-checking is crucial for ensuring the reliability of information obtained from Gemini.

If you've tried adjusting your prompt in several ways and are still not getting the desired output, what might be a helpful next step?
A) Keep trying the same variations of your prompt indefinitely.
B) Start over with a completely different approach to framing your request.
C) Assume that Gemini is intentionally trying to mislead you.
D) Ask a human expert for help instead of continuing to use Gemini.
Correct Answer: B)
Explanation: Sometimes a fresh perspective and a completely new way of asking can yield better results.

Chapter 14: The Future of Gemini and AI Collaboration

What is a potential emerging capability of AI language models like Gemini in the near future?
A) The ability to teleport physical objects.
B) Enhanced understanding of nuance and context in human language.
C) The development of true consciousness and emotions.
D) The complete replacement of human creativity in all fields.
Correct Answer: B)
Explanation: Improved understanding of language nuances is a likely area of advancement for AI.

How is the role of AI in creativity and productivity likely to evolve?
A) AI will become entirely autonomous and will no longer require human input.

B) AI might move beyond being just an assistant to becoming a more active collaborator in creative processes and a powerful tool for boosting productivity.
C) AI will primarily be used for entertainment purposes and will have little impact on professional fields.
D) AI's role will likely remain static, with no significant changes in the coming years.
Correct Answer: B)
Explanation: The trend suggests a more collaborative and impactful role for AI in both creative and productive endeavors.

What is essential for users to do to stay updated with the advancements in AI and continue mastering tools like Gemini?
A) Avoid learning about new AI developments to prevent feeling overwhelmed.
B) Rely solely on the knowledge gained from this book.
C) Embrace lifelong learning by following tech news, exploring online courses, and experimenting with new AI tools.
D) Assume that all future AI advancements will be automatically integrated into existing tools.
Correct Answer: C)
Explanation: The field of AI is rapidly evolving, making continuous learning crucial.

What are some potential future applications of AI in areas like writing and design?
A) AI will only be able to generate basic text and simple graphics.
B) AI could become more integral in creative workflows, potentially co-writing books or co-designing complex projects with humans.
C) AI will completely take over the fields of writing and design, eliminating the need for human professionals.
D) AI will only be useful for correcting errors in existing writing and designs.

Correct Answer: B)
Explanation: The potential for deeper collaboration between humans and AI in creative fields is significant.

Why will human oversight and critical thinking likely remain important even with more advanced AI?
A) Because AI will always be prone to making random errors.
B) Because humans will still need to guide the AI, evaluate its outputs, and ensure they align with goals and values.
C) Because AI will never be able to understand human emotions.
D) Because using AI is inherently unethical without human supervision.
Correct Answer: B)
Explanation: Human judgment and guidance will continue to be essential for effective and responsible AI use.

What is a good way for beginners to start staying informed about the latest developments in AI?
A) Immediately enroll in advanced university-level AI research programs.
B) Start by following reputable tech news sources, exploring introductory online courses, and engaging with AI communities.
C) Wait for a major breakthrough in AI before paying any attention.
D) Only rely on information shared through word-of-mouth.
Correct Answer: B)
Explanation: A gradual and accessible approach to staying informed is best for beginners.

What is the overall message regarding the future of AI collaboration conveyed in the final chapter?
A) Users should be fearful of AI taking over their jobs and creative pursuits.

B) The future holds exciting possibilities for enhanced creativity and productivity through collaboration with AI, emphasizing the importance of continuous learning and ethical considerations.
C) AI will eventually become so advanced that humans will no longer need to interact with it.
D) The future of AI is uncertain and not worth considering for beginners.
Correct Answer: B)
Explanation: The chapter aims to be forward-looking and encouraging about the potential of AI collaboration while highlighting key considerations.

As AI technology advances, what aspect of human interaction with AI is likely to become more important?
A) The ability to write complex programming code for AI.
B) The ability to provide clear guidance, critical evaluation, and ethical oversight of AI outputs.
C) The ability to completely trust AI's judgment without question.
D) The ability to build physical robots powered by AI.
Correct Answer: B)
Explanation: Even with advanced AI, human guidance and ethical considerations will remain paramount.

What is the ultimate takeaway from "Creating Gems with Gemini" regarding your journey with AI?
A) You have now learned everything there is to know about AI.
B) Your learning is complete, and no further exploration is necessary.
C) This book provides a foundation, and continuous experimentation and a critical approach will be key to unlocking the full potential of Gemini and other AI tools.
D) You should now be able to replace all human tasks with AI.
Correct Answer: C)

Explanation: The book aims to empower beginners to start their journey with AI, emphasizing the ongoing nature of learning and experimentation.

Appendix A: Prompt Library Sampler (Examples for Various Tasks)

This appendix provides a collection of prompt samples to help you get started with Gemini for various tasks discussed throughout this book. Remember to be clear, specific, and iterate on your prompts to achieve the best results.

I. Creative Writing & Storytelling

1. "Write a short story (around 200 words) about a cat who discovers a secret portal in its backyard."
2. "Generate three different opening sentences for a fantasy novel set in a city floating in the clouds."
3. "Develop a character profile for a detective who is also a retired opera singer. Include their motivations, flaws, and a key skill."
4. "Write a scene where two characters are having a tense conversation in a coffee shop. Focus on their unspoken emotions."
5. "Create a plot outline for a science fiction short story about a colony on Mars that loses contact with Earth."
6. "Write a poem about the feeling of autumn, focusing on sensory details like smell and sound."
7. "Generate a list of five unique names for a magical artifact in a medieval fantasy setting."
8. "Write a humorous dialogue between a robot and a human who are trying to assemble flat-pack furniture."
9. "Develop a myth or legend explaining the origin of a natural phenomenon like a rainbow or an echo."
10. "Write a short script for a commercial advertising a new brand of organic tea."

II. Research & Learning

11. "Explain the concept of photosynthesis in simple terms for someone with no science background."
12. "Summarize the main arguments presented in the article about the impact of social media on teenagers." (Provide the article text)
13. **"What are the key differences between the American Revolution and the French Revolution?"**
14. "List five interesting facts about the Amazon rainforest."
15. "Explain the theory of relativity in a way that a high school student can understand."
16. **"What are the major causes of climate change?"**
17. "Find information about the history of the internet."
18. **"What are the benefits of mindfulness meditation?"**
19. "Explain the process of how a bill becomes a law in the United States."
20. "Generate a list of reputable sources for learning about ancient Egyptian history."

III. Tone & Style Adjustment

21. **"Rewrite the following sentence in a more formal tone: 'Hey, what's up with the project?'"** (Provide the sentence)
22. "Make this paragraph sound more persuasive: 'We should consider using renewable energy.'" (Provide the paragraph)
23. "Write a short email in a friendly and encouraging tone to a colleague who is feeling stressed."
24. "Explain this technical concept in a simple and approachable style for a general audience." (Provide the concept)
25. "Rewrite this news headline to be more attention-grabbing and sensational." (Provide the headline)
26. "Make this piece of writing sound more academic and objective." (Provide the text)
27. "Write a short apology email in a sincere and empathetic tone."

28. "Rewrite this marketing copy to be more humorous and playful." (Provide the copy)
29. "Explain this complex legal term in plain English." (Provide the term)
30. "Write a tweet announcing this new product in an exciting and concise style." (Provide the product information)

IV. Mining for Code

31. "Write a Python function that calculates the factorial of a given number."
32. "Explain the following JavaScript code snippet: `function greet(name) { console.log('Hello, ' + name + '!'); }`"
33. "Debug the following HTML code: `<p>This is a <b>bold</p> text.</b>`"
34. "Translate the following Python code into Java: `for i in range(5): print(i)`"
35. "Write a simple CSS rule to make all paragraph text blue."
36. "Explain the concept of a 'for loop' in programming to a beginner."
37. "Generate pseudocode for an algorithm that sorts a list of numbers from smallest to largest."
38. "Write a SQL query to select all customers from a table named 'Customers' who live in 'Canada'."
39. "Explain what an API (Application Programming Interface) is in simple terms."
40. "Write a basic HTML structure for a webpage with a header, a main content area, and a footer."

V. Unearthing Insights - Data Analysis & Interpretation

41. "Summarize the following sales data: [Provide a list of sales figures over time]."
42. **"What are some potential trends you can identify in this list of website traffic data?** [Provide the data]."

43. "Explain what a 'correlation' means in the context of data analysis."
44. **"Based on this survey data [Provide the data], what are the most common responses to the question 'What is your favorite color?'"**
45. "Suggest a few possible reasons for the increase in customer complaints shown in this data: [Provide the data]."
46. "Explain the difference between the 'mean,' 'median,' and 'mode' in statistics."
47. **"Based on this data [Provide the data], what percentage of respondents answered 'Yes' to the question?"**
48. **"What are some initial insights you can draw from this set of student test scores?** [Provide the data]."
49. "Explain the concept of 'statistical significance' in simple terms."
50. **"Based on this data [Provide the data], what is the highest and lowest value?"**

VI. Designing & Brainstorming

51. "Brainstorm five different themes for a children's birthday party."
52. "Generate three possible names for a new coffee shop that emphasizes sustainability."
53. "Create a basic outline for a blog post titled 'The Benefits of Learning a New Language.'"
54. "Develop a user persona for a busy professional who wants to learn how to cook healthy meals quickly."
55. "Write a user scenario for someone using a mobile app to order groceries for the first time."
56. "Suggest some color palettes for a website that aims to convey trust and reliability."
57. "Brainstorm five unique features for a new type of smart water bottle."
58. "Create a basic structure for a presentation on the history of jazz music."

59. "Develop a user persona for a student who needs help with time management."
60. "Write a user scenario for someone trying to book a doctor's appointment online."

VII. Workflow Integration

61. "Draft a thank-you email to a client after a successful meeting regarding [Project Name]."
62. "Summarize the key points from the following email thread: [Provide the email thread]."
63. "Generate a few ideas for social media posts announcing a new product feature."
64. "Write a brief introduction for a report on the impact of artificial intelligence on the job market."
65. "Refine the tone of this email to be more professional and direct: [Provide the email]."
66. "Create a list of follow-up questions to ask after reading this research paper: [Provide the paper's abstract or key points]."
67. "Draft a concise meeting agenda for a 30-minute team discussion on [Topic]."
68. "Summarize the feedback received from customers in these survey responses: [Provide the survey responses]."
69. "Generate a template for a weekly progress report."
70. "Write a short announcement for the company intranet about an upcoming training session."

VIII. Troubleshooting

71. "I asked Gemini to write a story, but it's very generic. **How can I make it more specific and interesting?**"
72. "Gemini provided information about a historical event that seems incorrect. **How can I verify this?**"
73. "I'm trying to get Gemini to write in the style of Jane Austen, but it's not quite right. **What can I try?**"

74. "Gemini gave me a code snippet, but it doesn't seem to be working. **What are some steps I can take to debug it?**"
75. "I asked Gemini to explain a complex scientific concept, but the explanation is still confusing. **How can I get a clearer explanation?**"
76. "Gemini is providing biased responses on a particular topic. **How can I encourage a more balanced perspective?**"
77. "I'm trying to brainstorm ideas with Gemini, but I'm feeling stuck. **How can I get more creative suggestions?**"
78. "Gemini is summarizing a document, but it's missing some key information. **How can I improve the summary?**"
79. "I asked Gemini to write a poem, but the tone is off. **How can I adjust the tone?**"
80. "Gemini is giving me very short answers. **How can I encourage it to provide more detailed responses?**"

IX. Ethical Considerations

81. "**How can I ensure that the content I generate with Gemini is original and doesn't constitute plagiarism?**"
82. "**What are some potential biases that I should be aware of when using Gemini, and how can I mitigate them?**"
83. "**What are some guidelines for the responsible use of AI-generated content?**"
84. "**When is it important to disclose that I have used AI to generate content?**"
85. "**How can I use Gemini ethically in an academic setting?**"
86. "**What are some potential negative consequences of using AI for content creation?**"
87. "**How can I avoid spreading misinformation when using Gemini for research?**"

88. "What are the ethical considerations when using AI to generate creative works?"
89. "How can I be transparent with my audience about my use of AI?"
90. "What are the potential impacts of AI on human creativity and employment?"

X. Summarization

91. "Summarize the following article in three concise bullet points: [Provide the article text]."
92. "Provide a one-paragraph summary of the book 'To Kill a Mockingbird.'"
93. "Summarize the key findings of this research paper in simple terms: [Provide the paper's abstract or introduction]."
94. "Give me a brief summary of the main events of World War II."
95. "Summarize the customer feedback provided in these reviews: [Provide the reviews]."
96. "Provide a concise summary of the plot of the movie 'Inception.'"
97. "Summarize the key recommendations from this business report: [Provide the report's executive summary]."
98. "Give me a short summary of the main points discussed in this meeting transcript: [Provide the transcript]."
99. "Summarize the arguments for and against artificial intelligence."
100. "Provide a brief summary of the history of the internet."

Appendix B: Glossary of AI and Gemini Terms

This glossary provides definitions for some of the key terms related to Artificial Intelligence (AI) and specifically to Gemini that you might encounter throughout this book. Understanding these terms will help you better grasp the concepts and techniques discussed.

A

- **AI (Artificial Intelligence):** A broad field of computer science focused on creating machines that can perform tasks that typically require human intelligence, such as learning, problem-solving, [1] decision-making, and understanding language.
- 1. www.differencebetween.net
- www.differencebetween.net
-

B

- **Bias (in AI):** In the context of AI, bias refers to systematic errors or tendencies in the AI model's outputs due to flaws in the training data or the model's design. This can lead to unfair, discriminatory, or stereotypical results.

C

- **Context:** The surrounding information or details that help Gemini understand the meaning and intent behind your prompt. Providing sufficient context is crucial for getting relevant and accurate responses.

- **Constraint:** A limitation or specific requirement that you include in your prompt to guide Gemini's output. Constraints help focus the AI and ensure the generated content meets your specific needs (e.g., word count, specific format).

D

- **Debugging (Code):** The process of identifying and fixing errors or bugs in computer code. Gemini can assist with debugging by suggesting potential solutions to code problems.
- **Disclosure:** The act of informing others that content was generated with the assistance of AI. Transparency through disclosure is an important ethical consideration.

F

- **Fact-checking:** The process of verifying the accuracy of information, especially when obtained from sources like AI, which may sometimes generate incorrect details.
- **Fine-tuning:** A process of further training an existing AI model on a smaller, more specific dataset to improve its performance on particular tasks or within a specific domain.

G

- **Gemini:** The specific AI model that is the focus of this book. It is a powerful large language model developed to understand and generate human-like text and more.
- **Generic Response:** A response from Gemini that is broad, unspecific, or doesn't directly address the nuances of your prompt. This often indicates the need for a more detailed or refined prompt.

H

- **Hallucination (in AI):** A term used to describe instances where an AI model generates information that is factually incorrect, nonsensical, or not based on its training data.

I

- **Iteration:** The process of repeatedly refining your prompts and evaluating Gemini's responses to gradually achieve your desired output. This involves a cycle of prompting, reviewing, and adjusting.

L

- **LLM (Large Language Model):** A type of AI model trained on a massive amount of text data, enabling it to understand and generate human language with a high degree of fluency and coherence. Gemini is an example of an LLM.
- **Limitations (of AI):** The inherent constraints and weaknesses of AI models, such as a lack of real-world experience, potential for bias, and the possibility of generating inaccuracies.

M

- **Mitigation (of Bias):** Strategies and techniques used to reduce or minimize the impact of bias in AI models and their outputs. This can involve refining training data or adjusting prompting strategies.
- **Multimodal:** Refers to AI models, like Gemini, that can process and generate information across different types of data, such as text, images, audio, and video.

N

- **Natural Language Processing (NLP):** A field within AI that focuses on enabling computers to understand, interpret, and generate human language. Gemini utilizes NLP to interact with users through text-based prompts.

O

- **Originality (in the context of AI):** When using AI, originality refers to the user's responsibility to ensure that the final output doesn't infringe on existing copyrights and reflects their own unique contributions through modifications and refinements of the AI-generated content.
- **Output:** The text, code, or other content generated by Gemini in response to your prompt.

P

- **Parameters (in AI Models):** The adjustable variables within an AI model that are learned from the training data and determine the model's behavior and outputs. Large language models like Gemini have billions of parameters.
- **Plagiarism (in the context of AI):** Presenting AI-generated content as your own original work without proper attribution, especially if the content closely resembles existing copyrighted material.
- **Prompt:** The text instruction or question that you provide to Gemini to initiate a response or guide its output. The quality of your prompt significantly impacts the quality of the "gem" you receive.
- **Prompt Engineering:** The art and science of crafting effective prompts to elicit the desired responses from an AI model like Gemini. This involves understanding how to be clear, specific, and provide relevant context.

- **Pseudocode:** A simplified, human-readable description of the steps in an algorithm or computer program. It helps in planning the logic before writing actual code.

R

- **Responsible Use (of AI):** Utilizing AI tools and generated content in an ethical and thoughtful manner, considering the potential impact on individuals and society. This includes avoiding the spread of misinformation, respecting privacy, and being transparent.

S

- **Semantic:** Relating to the meaning or interpretation of words, phrases, and sentences. Gemini aims to understand the semantic meaning of your prompts to provide relevant responses.
- **Style (of Writing):** The distinctive way in which something is written, characterized by elements such as sentence structure, vocabulary, and tone. You can instruct Gemini to adopt specific writing styles.
- **Syntax (in Code):** The set of rules that govern the structure and grammar of a programming language. Correct syntax is essential for code to run properly.

T

- **Token:** The basic unit of text that an AI model like Gemini processes. Words and parts of words are often broken down into tokens. The length of prompts and responses is often measured in tokens.
- **Tone (of Writing):** The attitude or feeling conveyed in a piece of writing, such as formal, informal, humorous, serious, or persuasive. You can instruct Gemini to adopt a specific tone in its output.

- **Training Data:** The massive dataset of text, code, and other information that an AI model like Gemini is trained on. This data enables the model to learn patterns and generate responses.
- **Transparency (in AI Use):** Being open and honest about when and how AI is used in the creation of content or the execution of tasks.

U

- **User Persona:** A fictional representation of your ideal user, based on research and data. User personas help in understanding the needs, motivations, and behaviors of your target audience, which can be useful when prompting Gemini for design or content ideas.
- **User Scenario:** A narrative that describes how a user might interact with a product, service, or system to achieve a specific goal. These scenarios can help in designing user-friendly experiences and can be generated with the help of Gemini.

This glossary provides a starting point for understanding the terminology used in the world of AI and within this book. As you continue your journey with Gemini, you will likely encounter more terms, and we encourage you to keep learning and expanding your knowledge.

Conclusion - Your Journey to Becoming a Gemini Gem Creator

Congratulations! You've reached the end of "Creating Gems with Gemini - Mastering the Art of AI Interaction." By now, you've embarked on a fascinating journey, learning how to effectively communicate with Gemini to unlock its vast potential and generate high-quality outputs – those valuable "gems" we've been exploring throughout this book.

We started by understanding what AI and Gemini are, establishing a foundation for our exploration. You then delved into the crucial art of crafting effective prompts, discovering how clarity, specificity, and context are key to guiding Gemini towards your desired results. You learned the importance of iteration and refinement, recognizing that the initial response is often just the starting point for polishing your "gems."

From unleashing your creativity in writing and storytelling to mastering information through research and learning, you've seen how versatile Gemini can be. You've explored the nuances of adjusting tone and style, mining for code, and even unearthing insights from data. You've also discovered how to integrate Gemini into your existing workflows and brainstorm innovative ideas.

Crucially, we also navigated the ethical landscape of AI gem creation, emphasizing the importance of originality, bias awareness, responsible use, and transparency. Finally, you gained valuable troubleshooting skills to help you when your interactions with Gemini don't go as planned, ensuring that a "dry mine" doesn't halt your progress.

The goal of this book was to empower you, a beginner with little to no prior experience, to confidently interact with Gemini and produce meaningful results. We hope that you now feel equipped with the knowledge and practical skills to harness the power of this incredible AI tool for your creative, learning, and productivity needs.

Remember that the world of AI is constantly evolving. Gemini itself will continue to develop new capabilities, and the ways we interact with it will undoubtedly expand. The principles you've learned in this book – clear communication, iterative refinement, ethical awareness, and a willingness to troubleshoot – will serve you well as you continue your journey.

The true mastery of AI interaction is an ongoing adventure. Keep experimenting, keep asking questions, and keep polishing those "gems." The potential for what you can create and discover with Gemini is truly limitless.

Meet the Author - Laurence Svekis

"Creating Gems with Gemini - Mastering the Art of AI Interaction" is brought to you by Laurence Svekis, a passionate advocate for accessible technology and lifelong learning. With a background spanning various aspects of digital media and online education, Laurence has always been fascinated by the power of technology to empower individuals and unlock creative potential.

Observing the rapid advancements in artificial intelligence, particularly in the realm of large language models like Gemini, Laurence recognized a need for a beginner-friendly guide that could demystify the interaction process and enable anyone to leverage these powerful tools effectively. This book is born out of a desire to bridge the gap between complex AI technology and everyday users, providing practical, actionable advice to help everyone create valuable outputs.